THE INFERTILITY CROSSROADS
– When IVF fails

by

Heather Easton

Copyright © 2018 by Heather Easton

All rights reserved. No part of this publication may be reproduced, distributed, or transmitted in any form or by any means, including photocopying, recording, or other electronic or mechanical methods, without the prior written permission of the author, except in the case of brief quotations embodied in critical reviews and certain other noncommercial uses permitted by copyright law.

Published by WriterMotive
www.writermotive.com

This book is not intended as a substitute for medical advice. The reader should consult a physician on matters relating to his/her health, particularly with respect to any symptoms that may require diagnosis or medical attention.

Please sign our petition to promote change in the NHS and provide equal IVF treatment for all.

https://www.change.org/p/jeremy-hunt-fund-ivf-consistently-for-all-not-via-a-postcode-lottery

In loving memory of Eva, our beloved, beautiful cat and IVF companion

2006 – 17th May 2017

Table of Contents

Introduction 9

1. Questioning our fertility 11

2. IVF round 1 16

3. The day that changed my life (World War 3) 32

4. The start of the adoption process 36

5. Fork in the road 40

6. IVF round 2 (in a different country) 42

7. Picking up the pieces, moving on with adoption and the cat who saved us 54

8. Stress, illness, leaving work and renewing our vows 60

9. IVF round 3 (clinic number 3) 65

10. Hitting rock bottom, illness, surgery and facing the truth 68

11. Starting a petition 77

12. Restarting the adoption process and adoption breakdown 79

13. Finding myself again (weight loss, friends & something to look forward to) 82

14. The sudden loss of Eva 84

15. Surgery number 2 90

16. IVF round 4 and 5 with Donor egg and surgery number 3 96

17. Family perspectives 117

18. Deciding how and when to move on 121

Z. Resources that helped me 131

Introduction

Hello. I'm Heather.

My husband Mark and I have sat at the infertility crossroads many times. Are you sitting at the crossroads right now, unsure of which turn to take? We had choices: do we choose more IVF, or go down the adoption route, or face childlessness? We have faced all three aspects of the crossroads, and you will learn about our experiences in this book.

I want to reach out to everyone who has felt lost and engulfed by their infertility story. I want to help people to choose, and allow them to learn from our good and bad choices. I want to offer a moment of reflection for others where reflection is so desperately needed in the process. I want to extend a helping hand so that no one feels as alone as I did. By the end of the book you will know, at least, that one other person has felt some of what you are feeling and allow you to realise that it's OK to feel that way.

In my darkest moments I would browse the Internet looking for books, blogs, social media pages; trying to find someone or something to read that would give my soul, heart and mind the answers I was desperate to hear. I only managed to find one book about facing childlessness; and that book didn't speak to me and my particular situation. It seemed to say that if I chose the adoption pathway then I somehow didn't count, as I would still be a mother. I found this view harsh; after all, I would still be losing my biological link to my child, and that is an enormous loss in itself. There had to be a book that would help when you are at your most difficult time – the crossroad – the fork in the road, whatever you like to call it. A book that would answer the questions uppermost in your mind: can I keep going? What is my life going to look like in the future? My childhood memory of playing with baby dolls, re-enacting what my life in the future would look like, was shattered. Maybe you had the same image in your head: the family-sized house, the perfect family, and your natural children. There ought to be a book to help you now; now that your childhood dreams are shattered and you are heading into the unknown.

You might simply read the contents of this book and think: right; which chapter do I read first? Which one will give me the answer I so desperately need the fastest? However, I urge you to read the whole book from the beginning; our journey unravels the thinking process that we went through, and the steps we took to eventually reach the decisions that led to peace and happiness. I'm sure you are seeking happiness, too, and I believe that reading our story – our whole story – will help you to find the solution you are seeking. This is the story of an emotional and physical journey that was long and tiring, but eventually rewarding. I hope that this book will help you to identify where you are in your own journey, and find the right path, one that meets your own needs and expectations.

I hoped it would be therapeutic to write this book: for me, my husband and family. I can truly say it has been.

1. Questioning our fertility

My husband and I had talked about having a family ever since we first met; it was very important for both of us. I was on contraception for the first few years after we met; I decided to come off the contraception due to it having side effects for me. If I'm honest, we weren't the most careful of couples in the bedroom as the years passed, purely because we loved each other and would have been happy with a child in our lives at that point, but it did get us thinking.

Remember all the scaremongering your parents laid on you when you were a teenager? 'Now you must be safe and use protection because it's so easy to get pregnant!' Well, that started to play on our minds; if it's so easy to get pregnant, how come we aren't being blessed with a baby? And there was another issue that haunted our minds. My husband had surgery as a child to treat undescended testicles, and the problem was only resolved when he reached the age of eleven. We looked this up on the internet, curious as to any ill effects this could cause, and found that the problem, and the aftermath of the operation, can affect sperm quality and numbers. We also discovered that the NHS normally performs this operation on boys of around two years old, and not usually as late as eleven years old. What damage might have been caused? The worry started to set in.

Mark and I come from regular working-class families. I work as a nanny, because of my love for children, and Mark works as a HGV driver. He has always been interested in driving, cars and aeroplanes especially. We had no idea of the expense we would incur in our encounter with the world of infertility. It certainly was not one our everyday jobs could keep up with.

In winter of 2013, our infertility journey began, when I was twenty-four and Mark thirty-one. I saw a BBC news article reporting that a major chemist was now selling a sperm check test which promised to be 98% effective in detecting whether sperm count was low or normal, for the very reasonable price of £30. I remember, one cold dark winter's night, going to the chemist just before it closed, anxious to take the test and see if any of my husband's sperm parameters had been affected by his childhood experience.

We carried out the rather straightforward test and waited for the result. We were shocked when it came back: low sperm. Was the test right? Did we carry out the test right? An inner panic set in, followed by a different feeling on my part: I knew it! I just knew something wasn't right. It was a gut feeling. I will talk about gut feelings a lot in this book because I feel they are so important and can really lead us in life if we choose to listen to them.

All the focus was now on Mark, and we didn't know what to do. This was something new and out of our knowledge and comfort zone. We went back to the internet, to see who could give us a more detailed and accurate test and provide some answers. We found a private company in the West Midlands that do sperm analysis. I think the test was around £100; quite a jump up from the earlier test price but far more detailed. Mark received the results by email; they showed he was low in all categories analysed. The test results were accompanied by a rather brief email saying, please see your GP and buy male conception vitamin tablets to help improve your sperm parameters. We were disappointed that the clinic didn't call and offer some support, guidance and explanation, considering we'd just parted with the first large sum of money (at least it felt that way at the time; we soon came to realise it was very cheap compared to the sums we would have to part with later) on our infertility journey.

Mark wanted to try out the conception vitamins, with the hope of improving his sperm; we went, as a couple, to see the doctor. We told the doctor that we had been trying for two years; that we'd carried out these two sperm tests; and we also explained Mark's childhood history. The doctor was satisfied that we had a case for further investigation and referred us to our local hospital's Reproductive Medicine Unit. We were told there would be a waiting list and in fact we waited several months for our first consultation. Meanwhile the GP had suggested monitoring my own monthly cycles. We invested another £100 or so in a cycle monitor, which measured LH levels to see when I ovulated; it could also be used to carry out pregnancy tests, using a different attachment you could plug into the monitor. Getting up to pee at roughly the same time every morning and peeing on the very expensive sticks (£30 for a box!) was rather tedious. As the months went on a pattern emerged: in the eight months I used it, there were two months when I did not ovulate. I was convinced it was the machine; or that I didn't pee right on the sticks; or that I didn't pee on the sticks on the right day. Also, as time went on, making love to a schedule began to feel like a chore instead of a pleasure. I didn't want a schedule, it didn't seem natural. We both felt the same about that. I started to get disappointed every month, when it was just my period that would show up, and no surprise baby. I had to get over the disappointment and stay positive about the next month. But it was hard to stay positive: surely, if we were putting in the effort to try and conceive on the right days, our odds should have improved? Mark was conscientiously taking his vitamin tablets too. I had also started to notice that my periods would come at different cycle lengths.

There was a variation of three days in length. Back in the days when I was on Microgynon contraceptives I had a regular 28-day cycle; but looking back now I realise that's exactly what it was supposed to do (that's what it said on the tin) and therefore it was masking any potential problems.

In the summer of 2014 I faced another couple of medical setbacks. I had a smear test done and it turned out that there was evidence of CIN 2 cells. I was so scared. Precancerous cells, potentially on the way to becoming cancer! I was only twenty-five; it just didn't seem fair.

One of my friends had experienced this very problem at an earlier age and her diagnosis was worse. She lives in Scotland, which turned out to be very lucky for her; if she had lived in England I don't know if she would be with us today, because the testing age is twenty-five in England versus twenty at the time in Scotland. (To my disappointment, Scotland have since raised the age limit to twenty-five in the year 2016).

The biopsy of the cervix was the most painful thing ever! There was no pain relief and they removed a piece of tissue the size of a grain of rice out of my cervix; that might not sound a lot but, let me tell you, it felt horrendous. I was to be monitored every six months to give my body a chance to fight the CIN cells. I started taking vitamins to improve my immune system to help fight it.

It is extremely important that you go for your smear tests regularly; I can't stress this enough! I ended up battling these pre-cancerous cells for a couple of years.

But the problems didn't stop there. The next issue was that I was bleeding for a month solid, without any obvious reason, which naturally made me worry; so for the first time in our lives we phoned and booked an appointment with a gynaecologist at a private hospital. It cost £120 for a consultation in a place that seemed more like a hotel than a hospital, and with the best customer interaction we've experienced at any point. We were met in the waiting room with a hand shake. A long conversation followed, and then a quick scan, and another conversation; the upshot was that I would try the pill for a month to see if it would reset my body clock.

We were getting married that month and we were also dealing with a house which needed to be fully renovated; definitely not what the doctor ordered.

We had bought the house under the illusion that it just needed some light decorating. What followed was a nightmare – literally! It all started with an inaccurate home survey report and major problems with a leaking roof and a cowboy roofer. The whole affair ended up in court. We managed to claim £10,000 off the home survey company for their mistakes in the report but we were still left with a shortfall. We stayed in that house one year then sold it and moved into a new house, unfortunately not making any money on the deal. I won't belabour you with the whole terrible story but it was so stressful.

With all that going on, at the same time as we were getting to grips with our infertility problems – and getting married in September of 2014 – we couldn't have timed things any worse. We certainly didn't ask for all those problems with the house or the infertility but it just seemed that the bad luck kept on coming.

Our wedding day was beautiful; the sun shone, everything went just how we wanted it to; but we couldn't escape the feeling (a feeling we still have to this day) that our wedding day, and the special days around it, were somehow contaminated with the stress of the house and our medical problems. Stress we did not need.

2. IVF round 1

In the summer of 2015 we had our first appointment at our local hospital's reproductive clinic. I was quite excited and nervous; keen to get on with the tests and move on to find a solution. While we sat in the waiting room we were both given long forms to fill in about our medical backgrounds. The waiting room was quite full but quiet; no one spoke, which made for a very awkward atmosphere. There were patients of all ages, but we were by far the youngest (I was twenty-five by then, and Mark thirty-two). There was a fish tank in the corner of the waiting room, which was a hit with any children that came in. I did wonder why there were children in an infertility clinic: perhaps they were previous IVF babies, I thought. Or maybe the families were experiencing secondary infertility.

The clinic didn't run on time, which made the waiting feel even longer. If there is one thing that comes up again and again on our journey, it's waiting. Everywhere we've gone, and every process we've tried, has involved more waiting than anything else. It's as if they are trying to teach you to be patient, to remind you that this might be a long process. Whatever the reason, be prepared to wait; unless you have more money than problems, there is no fast track on the infertility journey.

Finally, we were called through to see a male doctor. He listened to our medical histories individually. I don't know why, but I had it in my head he would just do investigations into Mark's infertility, but I was wrong; he wanted to test me too. I had blood taken to look at different hormone profiles, as well as evidence of sexually transmitted diseases. This seems to be mandatory at all clinics: testing

The Infertility Crossroads

for Aids/Hep B/Hep C and possibly Chlamydia, Gonorrhoea and Syphilis. I had to have a swab taken vaginally to look at bacterial levels and possible infections, and a scan of my ovaries and uterus. The doctor suggested I pay for an Anti-Mullerian Hormones Test (AMH) which looks at the egg reserve in my ovaries. The doctor told us that the NHS didn't have funding for it, so we would have to pay, but he said it would paint a clear picture as to my egg reserve and my reproductive clock. We agreed to take the test, and I think it cost us £85. The blood was sent to London and we were told it would take a couple of weeks to get the results. Mark's testing involved a blood test and more semen analysis. We then arranged another appointment in a few weeks to discuss the results.

Results day was finally here! We went to the clinic together, putting our bravest faces on, and – again – waited a long time to be seen. We saw the same doctor; he was very matter of fact and showed little emotion when he gave us our results, which felt quite cold. First, we went through Mark's results, which I remember feeling anxious about. Would his sperm parameters have improved? Wow! To our surprise they had all improved to within normal range, except morphology (this refers to the shape and size of the sperm). I found myself thinking: well, there will still be millions of the right shaped sperm, so surely this was not a problem. I was reassured by the doctor, too; he was happy with the results – and Mark was grinning like a Cheshire cat. He was obviously feeling much better about his manhood than before; the exercise and conception vitamins had done the trick. I was so pleased for him. Then it was time for my results; I was feeling really laid back about them until the doctor started speaking. 'Your egg reserve is really low for someone of your age; the AMH test showed you have POI; that's premature ovarian insufficiency. It means your body doesn't have as many eggs left as it should for someone of my age.' The tears started to fall

The Infertility Crossroads

down my cheeks: I was stunned. The doctor handed me the tissue box as he continued to spout medical jargon at us. I stopped listening to what he was saying: I was in shock. I had never been so shocked in all my life. I was not prepared for this; we had both honestly thought it was my husband's sperm parameters that would be the issue. Mark was stunned too. I only began to focus on the doctor's words again when he started to talk about solutions, and the actions we could take. First, he talked about a laparoscopy, which is an investigatory operation to see if the fallopian tubes are open, and to look for any other issues around the ovaries and uterus. It involves an incision in the navel and further incisions either side of the pelvic region. He then told us we would need IVF. Specifically, we would need a version of IVF called ICSI. ICSI is when they pick the best sperm and inject them directly into the egg to fertilise it. This is very different from straightforward IVF, when the egg is placed in a petri dish and the sperm are placed around the egg, so the best sperm fight to reach and fertilise the egg naturally. He told us he recommended ICSI because he could pick the best sperm and eliminate the problem of poor morphology. As he was telling us about the process, he said, 'You don't really need a laparoscopy if we are bypassing the fallopian tubes anyway and retrieving your eggs surgically.' Although I wondered why he had mentioned the laparoscopy in the first place if he was recommending ICSI, I went along with what he said. Looking back now, I really wish I had had the laparoscopy at the very beginning of our journey. If it's offered to you, I highly recommend the operation; it may just bring you some much-needed answers.

When we first asked for help with infertility we were hoping that it would just involve some kind of sperm injection (a process called IUI) carried out at the time of ovulation, with all the good sperm only. But now, armed with all this new information, we found ourselves on

The Infertility Crossroads

course for the most invasive form of treatment: ICSI. What a shock!

During my time as a nanny I'd worked for several people who had IVF treatment and, clearly, it worked; they were older than me at the time so I was quite confident, given my age, that it would work for us, although we did read off the clinic's statistics that there was only around a 30-40% chance of getting pregnant by IVF/ICSI. The Doctor handed us leaflets about the procedure and told us to read up on it. Needles were my first thought. Ahhhhh! I hate needles, I absolutely detest them! I thought for a moment and turned to Mark and said, 'You'll have to give me all my hormone injections; there's no way I can inject myself!' We left the clinic dazed, with an appointment booked for an information session to go through the procedure.

We looked at dates to see when the clinic would have appointments available that would fit with my monthly cycle. You can't just start IVF on any day of the month; it depends on what protocol you are on and then the correct day of your cycle. It was a couple of months before we could start the procedure (yes, more waiting) because of availability and needing this information session first.

My head felt like it was in information overload. The POI diagnosis went round and round in my head; I felt like I was crumbling inside with heartache. I hadn't been given any leaflets or literature when I left the clinic after this momentous diagnosis. So I of course turned to Google. I found an organisation called the Daisy Network, which supports women with Premature Ovarian Insufficiency or Premature Ovarian Failure. I joined for the year for a small fee and felt supported by the women online; but it was like being in a secret bubble of support that my husband couldn't get involved in. I just kept it to myself and felt alone with my own diagnosis. I did talk to Mark about my fear of going through the menopause early. I felt like I was the only one I knew who had been through this. No one in my family had experienced anything like it. I'd never even heard of women in their twenties (or even younger) going through this until I found this support group. They did get me through the dark early days of unanswered questions and fear. I do wish the IVF clinic could have sat me down for an hour and talked to me about this diagnosis, and given me some literature to go home with.

A few weeks later we went for our information session. We already knew about most of the procedure from the leaflets, but we were still quite nervous about finding out all the details that it would entail. Hearing the words straight from the nurse's mouth confirmed everything and made it feel real. We had a nice nurse; she gave us a sharps box to put our needles in, and a repeat prescription so we could collect our medicine from the pharmacy within the hospital. Then she used some large posters on the drugs, and some dummy needles, to show us how to inject into the stomach. We were given a chart for ticking off our injections as we went along. Some needles involved just dialling the dosage in by a twisting action and pressing a button when ready to inject. These were my preferred option: 'no nonsense needles' as I would call them. The other type involved mixing powdered drugs into water in vials, and then sucking it out with a fatter needle; and then changing that needle tip for the smaller needle that was the one you would inject with. Mark and I cringed when we heard from the nurse that some people mistakenly injected with the fatter needle that was only supposed to be used for drawing up the medicine. Crikey! There was no way I would be making that mistake; the needle was several inches long and very fat. Most of the needles were an inch long, or slightly more, but very fine. We had a laugh with the nurse about the needle explanations, probably because we were nervous and we wanted to make light of a daunting process.

There was no clear idea from the outset of how the dosage would go up for these drugs, or how many days I'd be on them; I had to be monitored every few days with scans to see how the follicles were developing. This gave them an idea of how to tweak the drugs to make the most of my cycle. The follicles need to grow to 18mm before being viable for harvesting an egg. Equally, if they grow to over 25mm they won't be viable. There is no guarantee all follicles have eggs in them, and there's no way of knowing this until they do the egg collection. The procedure all starts with a baseline scan, which for me was on day three of my cycle.

A few weeks later we started the IVF protocol. For us personally it was a difficult time in our lives. We had sold the house we had just renovated (or our 'disaster house' as we like to call it) and we were now living with my parents for two months before our new-build house was finished, in the first week of October. We had most of our personal belongings crammed into the house and some at a friend's house. We didn't have much privacy in what we felt should be a private time. To top it all off my employer was making me redundant and putting the little boy I looked after into nursery. I was devastated because I loved that little boy and he, in his own way, was my biggest supporter, my best friend.

I worried about the mortgage and money in general and about finding a job, when all I was supposed to be doing was focusing on my IVF. The only *free* IVF attempt we would have. Where we live, there is only one free attempt at IVF on the NHS. If I still lived in Scotland (as I had from the age of three until the age of nineteen) I would have been entitled to three free attempts at IVF. I felt so much pressure for it to work; a lot of money would be needed if not and with all the other pressure on top it wasn't good for us. My family told me to put off the IVF, but I didn't want to; I had wanted a child for so long and I thought now was my opportunity. Who knew how far down the waiting list I could be put if I didn't try now. The other time critical factor in my circumstances was my depleting egg reserve; every month counted.

If you are reading this book and you haven't started IVF yet, or you are considering further attempts at IVF, please consider doing it at the most optimal time, where stress is at a minimum. Looking back now, I do regret the timing of things; but in all fairness I thought we would have moved house by then (unfortunately our house sale fell through three times and we had to wait a bit longer for the house to be built) and I didn't anticipate losing my job. Honestly, what's waiting a month or two if that makes you less stressed trying for your baby? Parting with thousands of pounds, or parting with a free attempt on the NHS, are difficult, especially when the IVF doesn't work and you find yourself asking, 'was I too stressed?' I will talk more about this later, but there's no point in blaming yourself, you can only give it your all.

Ok, so back to our story: day three of my cycle I had my baseline scan. Scans are all internal vaginal scans and, let me tell you, I soon found that there's no dignity in the whole IVF process. At this clinic you could be scanned by any nurse on any of your scan dates; I found this impersonal and awkward. I did get a small bit of tissue from a roll to put over my lower regions when I was having the scan, and I clung to this small shred of dignity where really I had none. I'm sure I'm not the only one who feels like this. They looked at my uterus and ovaries during this scan and gave me the ok to proceed.

We were asked if we wanted to take part in a study for hyaluronic acid binding sperm selection. We agreed to it but we don't know to this day whether we were in the control group or experimental group. There is a website I found on this trial and it says they will publish their results in autumn 2017; however, there are still no results at the time of writing. It would be interesting to know if the hyaluronic acid method is a better way to pick the sperm than by a lab technician just choosing the best looking, strongest swimming sperm. (For more information on this I will share the link at the end of the book.)

We also had the option of putting our embryos in a special incubator which would take pictures of them every ten minutes; this meant that if the cells divided wrongly at any point they could look back and see what happened and when. This was not free; it cost us £390 for the embryo scope. It was difficult spending that sum of money for the first time. Looking back we think it was well worth the money. Having your embryos recorded paints a real picture and gave us vital information about egg quality and embryo development. I highly recommend you consider using an embryo scope, at least for your first attempt.

We also signed a lot of legal paperwork about the use and storage of our sperm, eggs and potential embryos. All clinics do this as standard.

The nurse filled in our chart for the first time indicating the dosage of medicine I would be taking and asked me to start injections that night. Scary, but exciting! We had to do a lot of organising with Mark's employer to make sure he could attend IVF appointments and also to make sure he could do the injections at the same time every day. It was apparently crucial to do the injections at the same time every day. The first night of injections I remember crying in anticipation of the needle going in my stomach. I got myself all worked up because I didn't know what it would be like to be injected there. We are all used to having an injection in our arm at some point in our life, but the stomach is such a different area of the body.

One thing I found I was grateful for was the few inches of fat I could hold between my fingers; injecting into fat is much less painful than injecting into muscle. So that would be my role in all of this; I would hold the few inches of fat firmly, with two hands wrapped in tissue, and I wouldn't look; Mark would tell me when he was going to put the needle in. I was surprised to discover that most of the time the needle didn't hurt or I hardly even felt it; but then as he slowly started the injecting it would sting or burn. I would then apply pressure with my tissue to stop the medicine coming out again. I found that if the needle didn't have a drip of medicine on the end before going in my stomach it didn't sting as much; but remember, the needle needs to be clean and sterile. We did have alcohol wipes to hand but we just used a tissue (which probably goes against all hygiene rules!).

The relief once my first injection was over was enormous. I felt proud of myself and so did Mark; he'd never injected another person in his life. It started to become itchy and red and slightly raised; I started panicking and worrying. The next day I called the nurse's station and they agreed to swap my medicine and protocol. I was very relieved; I got to go on a shorter protocol which meant fewer needles.

We continued for days, repeating the injection at the same time and dose, until our next scan was due. I was still a bit teary and panicky about it all and Mark would always pick up on my tensions; sometimes he was really supportive but at others times he was anxious and difficult with me.

The more holes Mark made in me the more I began to look like a Swiss cheese. We joked about this. I would have

The Infertility Crossroads

the injection on alternate sides of my navel going forward. I started to accumulate tiny red dots everywhere, so Mark knew where not to inject the next time. I made this a priority and made sure Mark followed my rule.

We then researched acupuncture, as it was recommended to aid success; I started having this treatment privately along with this round of IVF. The acupuncture needles were fine, not at all sore in comparison.

After several more scans and upping our medicine dosage we incorporated a second injection a day. The job of the second injection was very important. It was to prevent me from ovulating; that was the last thing we wanted my body to do because we wanted the doctor to collect the eggs. We were also ordered to do a final injection 36 hours before egg collection; the purpose of this injection was to mature the eggs. It was made clear to us by the nurses that we had to get the timing spot on and not forget to do this injection. This injection pen lived in the fridge, so we had to take it out of our fridge and give it at midnight. I remember staying up late and feeling relieved it was our last one. I still had the same worries: 'I hope the needle's not too big or doesn't hurt too much'. I had had the other injections earlier, at 8 pm, so really I'd had enough of needles by now. I had been having injections for 12 days on this protocol. Looking back, I reckon that, between all the medicine, blood tests, and IV lines in my arms, on average I would have had 50 needles for one round of IVF. I have to say, considering how scared of needles I was, that I was extremely brave; and I think the same is true for everyone out there who's been through it: You are brave and I am proud of you, too. You should be proud of yourselves; the things we women have to go through are unreal. I applaud you even more if you were the one who gave yourself the injection; and well done also to the brave partners who stepped up and did the injections.

Egg Collection day: I was very nervous and didn't get much sleep the night before. Mark had the day off work. He was nervous too and had the added pressure of producing a sperm sample on the day: not just any old sample, but *the* sample, the one which, combined with my eggs, would make our baby. We had to be at the clinic and ready to go into theatre for 8 am, and we arrived early. The clinic was closed on egg collection day; it was the weekend and the waiting room and reception desk were empty. Only egg collection patients were there in the ward. We knocked on the door of the ward to get a member of staff's attention. I had my little bag with a nightie and slippers. Mark was so loving and supportive, not showing his fears. We glanced around the ward as we were assigned to a bed. We were definitely the youngest there.

In the ward there were six beds. I had the one nearest the door. I was asked to change in to a nightie and await further instructions. I could see the other beds starting to fill up with hopeful couples, including one Chinese couple who needed the hospital to provide a translator. The nurse came and told me I would be first to go in for egg collection because I had a latex allergy; it made sense, so they wouldn't forget or contaminate the equipment further down the line.

I was really nervous to see how many eggs I would get. Mark was very excited and loving towards me. He was called away to give his sperm sample and I said goodbye to him as I was called to theatre. I had to give my name, date of birth and address, and confirm my partner's details; of course they had to be 100% accurate when creating the embryos.

I left my slippers at the door and climbed on to the operating bed. There were a lot of people in the room, including the embryologists, who were in and out of the room, theatre staff, nurses, the consultant, and the anaesthetist. The big thing for me was the controversy over whether I would be asleep or not for the sedation. Some nurses said I'd be asleep and others not. I was adamant that I did not want to be awake or feel anything; after all, they were putting a needle through my vagina wall and into my ovaries to drain all the follicles and collect the eggs. Ouch!

I remember focusing on the ceiling a lot so I did not have to look at all the strangers in the room. Then the anaesthetist started asking me questions about my health and started to explain about putting me to sleep. I thought: I just need to get past the needle in my arm and that's the worst bit over. He was a pro at putting needles in and I hardly felt it. Then he started to put liquid through the tube and eventually the big white plunger of medicine to put me to sleep. I watched it go in and felt as if I was under the influence of something. I stared at the ceiling for ages and remember thinking: I'm keeping these eyes open as long as possible because I don't want them to start when I'm awake. It did take a while for me to go to sleep and the consultant asked me if I felt sleepy. I nodded. Thank goodness, I went to sleep, out for the count, for what seemed like ages but was only fifteen or twenty minutes.

When I woke I was being wheeled down the corridor and I drifted in and out of sleep until I was in my bay, with Mark beside me again. I repeated the same question about ten times, 'How many eggs did we get?' Mark answered, 'nine', and he was very amused by all my confusion and repeated questions; ultimately we felt happy because from the scans we knew we had somewhere around nine follicles and not all follicles hold eggs.

The embryologist came around to our bedside and explained that we got six eggs from my right ovary and three from my left ovary. She explained what they would do; we would have to wait and see if they fertilised by ICSI. We could call the clinic at any time, but they would call us if they had news. There was a curtain around my bed at this point while she spoke to us. However, she then went on to speak to the other five couples, behind their curtains, and we could hear all of their conversations.

They all got way more eggs than me and they were all ten to fifteen years older than me; I was by far the youngest there. I was hearing collected egg numbers from twelve to mid-twenties. We were both really upset by this; it was so insensitive for us to overhear this information. I felt inadequate with my low egg numbers. I was discharged shortly afterwards and Mark took me home to rest. I was cramping and had a small amount of bleeding, which stopped within a few hours. I was really tired from the sedation but we were really excited about the future; we were really hopeful I would get pregnant. We just had to wait for a call about how many eggs had fertilised. The call came the next day and we were told we had eight eggs which were mature enough to use and out of the eight, five had fertilised. So now we were back to the waiting game, to see how many would make it to day five, blastocyst stage. We were on tenterhooks for those days. We called in a few days later to see how things were going and we were told there were two developing to blastocyst stage. The other three embryos had quickly arrested; this means they didn't make it, they either weren't continuing to grow or their cells weren't dividing as they should for a healthy embryo. We were really anxious. I remember those days as being really difficult; but we still had hope.

Finally the day arrived and we were called in for embryo transfer, back to the same ward and operating theatre for the procedure. We were really excited! As I took residency in my bed the embryologist came to see us. She explained they would be transferring one blastocyst that day, one that looked a good candidate; the other one wasn't looking as good but they would try and develop it in the lab for another day and, if it was successful, try and freeze it in storage. We were told that only a small percentage of people have enough eggs for freezing; we were a bit surprised to hear that as we thought it was more common. Maybe she was giving us the facts, or maybe she was just trying to make us feel better. We were disappointed but we still hoped the other egg might make it.

We were called in for the embryo transfer; Mark came in with me and held my hand. There was no sedation offered for the transfer. They used a speculum, then a catheter and ultrasound to guide the catheter through the cervix and into the womb where the embryo would be placed. I had to have a full bladder for the embryo transfer so of course I felt like I needed the toilet the whole time; with everything else that was going on I was really uncomfortable. The nurse was trying to distract me by comforting me; stroking my leg (which was up in a stirrup) and holding my hand. I remember feeling quite comforted by that. They showed us our embryo on screen. That was exciting, a touching moment for us. Mark was smiling the whole time. I remember the part where they checked the catheter and they said it was definitely in my womb because the catheter was clear. We felt really happy and I was itching to go back to the ward to rest for half an hour and have a wee. It did cross my mind that if I had a wee it might fall out. Of course that's not true, but it crosses most women's minds when they go through this procedure. We were really in love for the next half an hour, full of hope that our embryo would turn out to be a beautiful baby; it was a precious time for us. The doctors put a lot of emphasis on relaxing in the coming two weeks, while we waited to be able to take a pregnancy test. I was to take pessaries and tablets to support the pregnancy every day, along with prenatal vitamins.

The Infertility Crossroads

The two-week wait – oh it was awful! The second week was worse than the first. I was at my parents' house, unemployed, trying to relax and trying not to think about getting a job so I could focus on us and our embryo. During the first week I found it easier to occupy myself and my mind but as the second week came my body started to change; things seemed different and I was on the internet every five minutes Googling my symptoms. I really thought good things were happening; in fact, I was convinced, and so was Mark. I wished that time would pass faster, instead of running at what seemed literally a snail's pace. We had been given our date to go into the clinic to take a pregnancy test but two days before that date I started bleeding and I was really worried. The day of the test I woke at 4 am in full-blown agony. Scrunched up in the foetal position, bleeding really heavily, I could barely move. I hobbled to the bathroom to sort myself out; I was crying my eyes out because of the shock of waking in this state, the dread and what I could only describe as feeling like I was having a miscarriage. I was in agony. I woke Mark and we were both upset. I just knew then that it had failed to turn into a beautiful pregnancy. I was still really upset at breakfast and couldn't see the point in going to the clinic. I had taken a test at home that morning and it was negative. We were heartbroken! I can't describe the pain. We went to the clinic anyway and they confirmed it was a no; they could see how upset we were and let us exit out the back door of the clinic – I felt embarrassed because I was in floods of tears. The nurses were trying to be as nice as possible. I'll never forget it; it was a sunny day and we were standing in the car park hugging each other and I was crying. We couldn't believe that it hadn't worked.

Our only free chance on the NHS was gone. The image of us being a happy family was gone and I was left in pain and bleeding. The pain really crushed us emotionally. We were both lost for words, unsure what to say to each other.

In the days that followed my focus quickly shifted from the loss and pain to what we should do next. I had read that women are often quite fertile after a failed IVF so I bought a sensor to wear on my skin (to the side of the body where your bra sits) that constantly takes your temperature throughout the day and night. The information is recorded on a graph which is communicated to the company and they tell you when you are ovulating and what your fertile window is. It was really expensive – £500 – and after only one month my readings weren't making sense and I didn't feel like it was worth the money; I sent it back and got my money back.

I was starting to lose direction. Neither of us knew what to try next to produce a family. It was starting to become a minefield we were wading through; something always seemed to blow up in our faces and there was disappointment at every turn.

3. The day that changed my life (World War 3)

It was now October 2015 and we had moved into our new house, which was just bliss compared to the old one. It was shiny and new and felt very calming, with its nice outlook and lovely neighbours. At least one of our problems was solved: a fresh start in a new housing scheme and at least one less thing to worry about. We could now focus entirely on having a baby.

We were due for our follow-up consultation after the failed IVF, which took place a month after the original procedure. I wondered if they do that so you have time to grieve and reflect a bit; or because they are simply too busy to fit you in sooner. To us it felt a long time away, when all we wanted was answers.

We went to the clinic feeling very anxious. The doctor was running half an hour late and this just added to our heightened sense of anxiety. When we sat down he apologised and explained he'd been dealing with some kind of emergency. He took out our notes and proceeded to read them; he wasn't actually the doctor we saw at our IVF, he was just our consultant at the start of the referral process, which made it all the more confusing and impersonal. He paid particular attention to the embryologist's notes and started to talk through the embryos one by one; I remember him saying that they all started to arrest very quickly, and that wasn't what they would be hoping to see in the development of the embryos. The egg quality was not good, he explained. Everything started to become a blur of negative comments. He was talking about me; my body had produced those eggs. I felt I wasn't good enough. I felt

The Infertility Crossroads

I wasn't capable of succeeding in making a baby. I started to cry. I just couldn't stop the tears falling down my face. The doctor handed me the tissue box and continued to talk in medical jargon which was difficult to understand. I then heard him say, 'You will need a donor egg for a chance at success.' Immediately I felt as if my world had just ended. My heart just broke. I couldn't believe what I was hearing. My eggs weren't good enough! He told me that I would hit menopause by the age of thirty-eight. I couldn't believe how young that was. The doctor then had the cheek to say he couldn't take any more questions and that he had to go to his next meeting. So he left us there, contemplating the worst news of our lives, and then we were punted out the door. That meeting shouldn't have been rushed; he could have at least once offered some condolence or sympathy. I wasn't crying at this point; I was in shock. Mark had to rush off to work; he was running late but clearly not in any frame of mind to go to work. I drove back to my parents' house, crying as I drove, and as soon as I got in the door I collapsed, sobbing my eyes and heart out; I couldn't speak to my mum. She kept saying over and over again, 'what's happened, what's happened?' She obviously realised it was not good news at the meeting and had to sit me down and calm me down before she got a word out of me. I will never forget that day; I collapsed in her arms, sobbing my heart out. It was the lowest point in my life.

I don't actually remember my mum's response, other than her trying to calm me.

A few years later I watched a movie called *Patriots Day*, about the Boston Marathon bombing. There was a scene in the movie that helped me make sense of that day when I sobbed my eyes out. Mark Walberg's wife in the movie is unable to have children and he describes the day she found out. It is a gripping scene that perfectly sums it up; his character says that it felt like World War 3, and that point stuck with me. He goes on to say, with regards to terrorism, 'All you have to fight back with is love', and I believe the same applies to being childless, or in any terrible situation or circumstance. Hug the ones we love a bit tighter and show strength through love; for the people and things in life we most cherish.

It's funny, but I have found myself going to a movie several times since our fertility problems, movies that by the title or trailer were totally unrelated to infertility, and randomly in the movie there would be a heart-rending scene about someone's fertility issues and childlessness; it would take me back and I'd be stuck in the cinema watching the whole scene play out, forced to face the reality of my own situation. This always feels awkward for Mark and me. It's just like they say; you can't hide from your own problems, you have to face them to get through them. Another movie I recall was *The Longest Ride*, which I just thought was about horses and romance, but there it was right in the middle of the movie, the theme of childlessness. I do recommend you watch these kinds of movies, though; I think it is good for you to face your own grief.

After that meeting we decided to call a separate meeting with the professor that we had paid extra money to so we could use the embryoscope. It definitely was money well spent; it gave us the best insight into our egg quality and allowed us to meet her for a review of her findings. It also allowed us to get a copy of the video from the embryoscope, showing our embryo's development.

The professor told us my eggs were unlike any she had seen before. She called me 'special', which actually just made me feel that I was special in a bad way. She told us that when they tried to put the pipette of sperm into the egg the outer layer of the egg didn't bounce back and close properly. In other words, it didn't have the proper elastici-

The Infertility Crossroads

ty. What made my eggs unlike any she had seen before was a strangely looped outer appearance. She suggested that maybe I had a protein missing, one I was born without. The question that immediately came to my mind was whether all my eggs would be of this quality. She told us it was like looking for a needle in a haystack to find one egg of good quality. She suggested we could try half ICSI and half IVF next time; perhaps that would show if allowing the sperm to swim into the egg by itself would be less damaging than a technician using a pipette to puncture the wall of the egg. And of course, just like the other doctor, she mentioned donor eggs or adoption. We appreciated her knowledge, her calm demeanour and the time she spent with us. It allowed us to talk quite freely and explore options without me getting upset. However, I did cry when we left the meeting; yet again, the donor egg and adoption words had been used and it seemed so final, a sign that we would not have our own children. I was now twenty-six, and this was my prognosis.

4. The start of the adoption process

It was now Autumn 2015 and, with a negative prognosis and with no interest from either Mark or myself in going down the donor egg route, we started looking into adoption in the UK (I wanted to make it clear that we live in the UK because I know if you're reading this, for example, in America it's a very different process, which costs a lot of money. In the UK, adoption does not cost money, except maybe a small fee for a medical, around £100).

I went onto the internet and discovered that the area where we used to live was holding information sessions on adopting and fostering. We had heard that it was not a good idea to adopt from where you live currently in case you bump into the birth parents. In fact, if you adopt a baby in its first year you are supposed to stay out of the area they were born in completely, until your baby's face has changed and become somewhat less recognisable. The area where we used to live had a higher level of children going into care, so it seemed the obvious choice. It took a bit of persuading for Mark, but we went to the event.

The adoption information session was a really relaxed, informal gathering of different types of social workers: matching social workers, child social workers and fostering team members. They had lots of tea and biscuits and there were a few other people there who were interested in adoption and fostering. It wasn't a large gathering; there were maybe 15 people in total. My first impression was that they were all really friendly. They paired anyone interested in fostering with the people who dealt with fostering and we were spoken to by the adoption team as a group. They gave us a huge amount of information about the process, and also the kinds of children up for adoption, with examples of what they might have gone through and what they would need from us as adopters. They talked about the criteria for adopting. There was also the option of fostering to adopt. We could tell that one social worker was really keen on us and she knew we were interested. At the end of the session we were given a leaflet and there was a phone number we could call if we wanted to start the process. It gave us a lot to think about. Mark was really positive and upbeat after the information sessions; it had opened his eyes and he had really enjoyed it.

Mark and I had long conversations over what we knew so far about the adoption process and if we felt we could adopt. By January 2016, we came to the conclusion this was for us, and we started the adoption process. We decided to choose this path because we were confident in my ability to look after children, especially children with challenging needs, as we had been told this could arise. We felt this was our option to have a family. This would also give my body a break from any further strain from IVF drugs and procedures; and ultimately this process would result in a child for us, without the major uncertainty that further IVF would bring.

We said goodbye to our fertility by planting a new plant in the garden and held a personal ceremony, just the two of us.

Then we started the process; I called the number on the leaflet we had been given and the lady who knew we were keen at the meeting remembered us.

We had a home visit at the start of January, where we had to fill in forms, and the social worker chatted to us and looked around our home. We quickly started to understand that there would be a lot – and I mean a lot! – of paperwork involved. It was now all about proving to social services that we were honest, decent people with the right intentions. We had to have disclosure checks done, and medical checks (involving a trip to our local GP where they carried out some general health checks and our medical history was noted). Then there were the endless references that needed checking. They had to write to past employers and personal references as this was also necessary. As a nanny I had worked for many families and the list was very long, but they did as they said and wrote to all my past employers. As we had said we were interested in fostering to adopt too, we had the medical check-ups paid for by the council. Most of the paperwork was done by the social workers, in the background, and we often had to wait weeks for checks and such like to come back.

In case you want to know about fostering to adopt, it is a new process. Babies coming through the care system, where there is a minimum 85% certainty they will go on to be granted adoption by the courts, can be fostered by prospective adoptive parents until such times as they are granted permission to adopt the child. This process has its challenges: for example, the child may be given contact with the birth parents, as often as once a week, at a contact centre, which brings with it the uncertainty that, at any moment, the child could be given back to its birth parents or an extended family member. Most of the cases for foster to adopt are those where the parents have had their children taken off them before and their circumstances haven't improved; so there is a high probability that it would be deemed safer and in the child's best interest for them to be adopted. Naturally, the social services want children adopted as fast as possible when that decision has been made, because it benefits the child. The foster to adopt process is supposed to support this process. The positives of the process are that you could have this child placed with you from birth, and watch your child grow up from birth, without the transition of moving from a foster carer to the adopter. The fewer transitions for the child, the more it benefits the child.

The process as a whole is supposed to take between four and six months to meet government guidelines. We really wanted to go on holiday before we adopted, so when we came back from a weekend city break we booked a holiday to Florida, which we were excited about. Some of our checks started to come back positive and things were moving forward. We were cleared to start the adoption training, which was a two-day intensive adoption training session.

5. Fork in the road

The adoption process had started to become more real until all of a sudden one evening Mark opened up and told me that he had changed his mind; he had a strong feeling that we should try IVF one more time. What if the doctors were wrong? How did we know all our eggs were of poor quality? Was the hospital the right place for us? He just couldn't close the door on the idea of us having a baby yet.

Added to that, there seemed to be a lot of scaremongering in the adoption process; the professionals seemed to tell us negative things at every meeting. They told us about the challenges; the varieties of challenging children and the scary scenarios we could come across. It really did feel like we were being discouraged from carrying through with the adoption process. Looking back on it now, I would like to see more positives being raised instead of putting people off; they definitely succeeded to some degree in putting us off the idea in the early initial stages.

I had no choice but to support my husband and agree with him that we would have another go at IVF. I would do anything for my husband. After the shock of him telling me all this, I really did allow myself to get excited again at the prospect of IVF working and us having our own baby. I told him if we were going to do this we had better organise it pretty quickly. We told the adoption agency we couldn't make the training session; we knew they were held every couple of months, so we planned to make the next session if the IVF didn't work out. We never told the adoption agency what we were doing because if they knew they would have kicked us off the scheme; they like at least six months to have passed after any IVF or trying for a

The Infertility Crossroads

baby to give the couple time to grieve. We didn't want to close any doors at this point in our life so we decided to keep the adoption door open, while keeping our fresh attempt at IVF hidden from the social workers. We also felt that it wasn't fair to put a six-month ban on the process, it seemed arbitrary; after all, some people can move on quicker than that and some people take longer. It depends on your own circumstances, what you have been through, what you feel and what the reality of the situation is. We all react differently and a 'one size fits all' approach didn't seem right to us.

6. IVF round 2 (in a different country)

After Mark's change of heart and with my renewed willingness to try IVF again, I started to research IVF clinics. Online, I found a doctor in Greece who had worked with the famous IVF pioneer, Dr Robert Winston. The website looked really good; it had lots of information and he seemed to be quite a famous doctor for infertility in Athens. There was another clinic we looked at too, but the website wasn't so good with information and I didn't feel as confident with choosing that clinic; this link to Dr Robert Winston sounded really promising and the success rate for the clinic was apparently really high.

The next step was funding our trip. I had to write down all the costs which I had researched; flights, hotel, car hire, medication, UK tests which needed to be done (and results sent to the Greek doctor before our trip), food, miscellaneous expenses, and IVF treatment costs. This came to a total of £6,000. The trip was to be three weeks because the IVF protocol was so long. Of these costs the medication was about £1,000 and the IVF treatment cost £1,900. Pre-trip tests came to over £500. We had to get blood tests, I had an ultrasound scan, and Mark had a semen analysis. The rest of the money spent on the cost of the trip itself. I called my parents and begged them for some money to help pay for the trip. They were shocked to hear of our change of heart but understood. They could see I had done a great deal of research and they really wanted us to be happy and have a miracle baby. After several pleading phone calls they kindly agreed to give us the money to fund the medical side of things; we would have to find the rest of the money ourselves.

The Infertility Crossroads

One major obstacle we had to overcome was cancelling our Florida holiday; we couldn't afford to do both and, if I fell pregnant, I wouldn't want to fly, or be able to get the time off work. We took a big hit by cancelling our holiday and lost £500. Mum and Dad were disappointed we weren't going to travel with them to Florida. It made Mark feel really angry that the travel company were keeping half our fare, but we had to accept the reality of the situation.

There was no going back now; we were committed to the trip. We were really lucky to have such understanding and supportive employers, who could give us the time off with short notice for such a long period of time; more so for my employer since it would mean finding alternative childcare for that time.

A few weeks passed and then we were off to Athens for IVF. The night before we left I got to fulfil one of my dreams of a lifetime, seeing Mariah Carey in concert. I was so excited I can't tell you! I went with my mum and we got great seats six rows from the front. I thought I would draw energy from her strength and her music for my trip. We had an amazing night, one I'll never forget. The concert went on till late and mum stayed over at our house afterwards.

Early in the morning my dad drove over to pick us all up and we headed for the airport, a few hours away. I loved the concert but let me tell you I did not get much sleep that night at all and I was completely shattered, to the point that as we were approaching the airport I broke down and started crying. I was emotionally drained and physically drained. I was so scared about going to another country for three weeks to have medical treatment. I was kind of trusting in the fact that my husband once had laser eye surgery, before I met him, in a foreign country, and he said it was all fine; but I still felt a bit scared about everything. I told myself I just needed to get there and suss out the clinic, then everything would be fine. I realised my emotional upset was because I was leaving the safety of my parents, even though I had my husband by my side. I guess we all have that inner child in us saying our parents will protect us always.

Our flight was quite early in the morning, so by the time we got to Athens it was lunchtime; we hired a red Fiat Panda (the cheapest car for rent) and headed straight for the clinic. Mark drove very well considering how scary the traffic and drivers were! Lots of people were weaving in and out of traffic on mopeds. We arrived at what looked like a very modern building and upon entering met the – very friendly – doctor and had a scan. The doctor told us to come back on Wednesday, two days later, when I would be on day two of my cycle.

Meanwhile, our mission was to source the IVF drugs from a local pharmacy. In Greece, you don't need a doctor's prescription, like in the UK; you just have to know the medicines you require and you can buy or order them over the counter. It seemed very relaxed in terms of rules. After a few hours at the clinic and all the travelling we headed for our first hotel, the Melia, and had dinner there. We were starving because we'd missed lunch. The hotel was lovely and the restaurant staff were very friendly.

I really want to give a detailed account of our trip abroad for IVF, in case anyone looking into this wants more information on the kind of schedule we had, and also to illustrate just how much we have been through on our journey.

Tuesday – We went to a local supermarket to buy some water bottles and stayed for lunch at a Starbucks we found next to the supermarket. In the afternoon we went in search of a pharmacy; we couldn't find the one we were looking for, which had been recommended by the clinic, but instead we came across a small pharmacy run by a friendly couple. We told them our predicament and how we urgently needed to source these drugs. We placed our order and hung around the area for an hour. Sure enough, an hour later a man on a scooter arrived at the pharmacy with a plastic bag containing our drugs. Bam, there goes £1000 on drugs; but we were very grateful because we'd discovered during our search that there was a shortage across the whole of Athens of IVF drugs. That night we had dinner at a local restaurant a short distance from the hotel; we had pasta, followed by cakes at a patisserie. By now we were starting to feel at ease in Athens and we couldn't have asked for nicer, friendlier locals.

Wednesday – In the morning we went to the clinic and had a blood test and a scan to see if I was ready to start the IVF cycle. I got the go-ahead and I was told to start taking Gonal F that night at 8.30 pm. We moved hotels from the Melia to the Radisson Blu Park Hotel, as our free night's stay using points at the Melia had run out. Again we found super friendly staff at the Radisson Blu Park hotel. Unfortunately, I developed a bad cough so we got medicine at the local pharmacy (yes, there seemed to be pharmacies everywhere!). We also ordered more fertility drugs. We had lunch and dinner at the hotel because we felt the food was the kind of food we would normally eat back home, which we found really comforting. I had a bad night, coughing, and went through lots of honey and lemon.

Thursday – We walked for 30 minutes into the historic centre of Athens. Along the way we stopped at a department store and some shops. We had lunch at the Hard Rock Café, where we bought a teddy which had 'Athens' printed on its t-shirt; we hoped we would be able to give it to our miracle baby. On the walk back we stopped at a department store café, because it was a really hot day and refreshments were needed. The funny thing is, some of the locals were wearing jackets, but we as Brits were not used to the hot weather (it was in the mid-twenties). We went to pick up our drugs from the pharmacy but after a mix-up on the order we had to take a cab to another pharmacy to get them. The taxi was a very reasonable price, I remember, compared to UK taxis. It was late now, so dinner at the hotel.

Friday – Today we went to the clinic first thing. I had a blood test and scan which showed two follicles in each ovary. Our doctor gave us a schedule explaining how to up the Gonal F dosage in increments each day, and started us on the second drug the following Sunday. Today was a Greek bank holiday so the shopping mall was closed. We went to the zoo instead, after much palaver with the sat nav. We enjoyed seeing the elephants and monkeys, and ended up in the reptile house; then it started to rain really heavily. The reptile house started to flood. No one could get out until the rain subsided. We were stuck next to a giant crocodile, right beside its pen! After half an hour of waiting the rain subsided and Mark had to give me a piggy back over the water because I had sandals on; it was quite funny. As we left the zoo through the turnstile I stood on the turnstile's steel bars to stop my feet from getting wet. Exhausted from our trip to the zoo, I had a nap in the afternoon and we went to TGI Fridays for dinner, followed by room service late at night. The bill for food was starting to mount up.

Saturday – The shops were open again today so we went to the Golden Hall, a very upmarket shopping centre, and McArthur Glen, a shopping outlet. I had to buy some more honey for my throat, but I didn't buy any clothes because they were all so expensive. I had my eye on a pair of camper shoes which I will buy tomorrow at a different shoe shop which has them in stock. At the McArthur

Glen, Mark accidentally ordered too much McDonalds with a coupon which was repeated three times on the back of a receipt. So we ended up with three drinks, three lots of fries and six burgers. It was so funny. There was no way we were going to eat all of that food. That night was the fourth injection of Gonal F.

Sunday –We had a lot of time in Athens that needed to be filled while we waited for my follicles to grow (yes, yet more waiting) so today we went to the Archaeology Museum in the morning; it was very grand and busy. Afterwards we changed hotel rooms to a quieter one. Then lunch at TGI Fridays followed by a cake at the bakery. We had a snooze later in the afternoon and a hotel dinner. Mark ventured to the hotel gym in the evening but came back in time to inject me with a higher dose of Gonal F and the first injection of Orgalutran, which gave me a small rash around the injection site. Tomorrow was a big day at the clinic as we would find out, hopefully, when egg collection would begin.

Monday – We went to the clinic, and after a long wait we had a scan revealing we had six large follicles and a few small ones. A bit disappointing; we didn't have a date for egg collection yet but we were to go back Wednesday. I was starting to feel really uncomfortable by now as both my ovaries felt sore. We went to the Golden Hall for lunch and then a fantastic drive out by the shoreline. We found an exclusive 5-star hotel where celebrities and politicians stay, called Astir Palace Resort, in Vouliagmeni. We hung out at the hotel and liked it so much we booked in for the Monday and Tuesday. We knew we could cancel our other hotel free of charge for those days. We needed a beach break to get away from the hustle of the city and to relax at that important stage of the treatment. We felt we had seen a whole other side to Greece today and we had dinner in the park by the seaside as the sun went down.

Tuesday – Today we went on the big red bus, sightseeing, and it was sunny, 19 degrees Celsius. I was really sore and uncomfortable in my ovaries. We hopped on and off the bus and I picked up the camper shoes at the other store. Stops included the Acropolis and Pireus to see the marina and cruise terminal. My cough was a little better but I needed a nap again in the afternoon. We went back to the first hotel, the Melia, for dinner, as we had started to become friends with the waitress there. The evening injections were the highest dose yet: 550 IU Gonal F. We used a glass bottle to put all the used needles in; I'm sure It made us look like junkies to the maid who cleaned our room, so we had to explain about all the medicine in the fridge to the staff. Tomorrow we are going to the clinic and really hoping for egg collection Friday.

Wednesday – We had good news from the clinic; we would have egg collection on Saturday and transfer the embryo on Monday. We were seen quickly today for blood tests and a scan. We were told I would have Intralipids and a scan on Friday. Intralipids is a liquid on a drip into your arm which is supposed to help suppress your immune system and prevent it from attacking or rejecting your embryo. Later, we had lunch at the Golden Hall again and we walked to a nearby mall for a look around. By now we were getting a bit bored and our bills were mounting up. We decided, using the free wifi at the Golden Hall, that we would change our flights and go home half a week early, so our trip would be a total of two and a half weeks instead of three – this would save us some money. We had our date for embryo transfer and we didn't need to be in Athens after that. I worried about flying straight after having the embryo transfer but the doctors said it would be fine. I decided it was best to rest the day after transfer and then go home the following day. Changing the flights cost us a bit more money but we figured it would save us money in the long run, compared to the cost of hotels and eating out. The weather was sunny and warm so we went back to the garden café by the sea for a walk and some food.

Thursday – The last day in March and last day of injections! What a relief! I was ready to pop. The injection was upped to 600 IU of Gonal F and there were two more injections to go. Ovitrelle, at midnight, to mature the eggs, was the third injection. I had totally had enough of needles by now and my stomach had had enough of them too. We went to the new Athens acropolis museum today, which was very modern, and ate lunch on the terrace café. Back for a nap at the hotel and ice cream. Back to TGI Fridays for dinner and we saw the guy from the hotel with his friends, so we all got chatting. In the evening I watched the movie *The Intern* on my iPad. It was important to have little things to pass the time when we were waiting for medical treatment and I felt too sore to be constantly walking around.

Friday – We went to the clinic for 9.30 am for my Intralipids, which I had in the recovery room. Nine other women were there, all for different treatments. The lady doing the Intralipids was very nice to me. When the Intralipids were hooked up to my arm I could taste this strange taste at the back of my throat and a feeling of butterflies in my stomach. The drip took an hour and a half to finish and Mark had to wait outside in the waiting area because no men were allowed in. I was very hungry and tired when I left and a bit emotional about the next day. I had lunch and a nap then we went to Lidl in the afternoon. In the evening we said goodbye to our favourite waitress, at dinner in the Melia; she was called Fotini. She was pregnant herself and she wished us good luck, and we wished her well too.

Saturday – Egg retrieval day! The clinic was quiet today, probably because it was a Saturday. I was the first person in. There were only three women there for treatment, and two doing Intralipids. Surprisingly, I felt calm; I was familiar with the recovery room now and reassured that the staff were all lovely. My arm hurt as I fell asleep under the sedation, and I woke with tears in my eyes, very tired but feeling fine otherwise. The anaesthetist was standing over me, trying to reassure me, and told me that some people don't wake well, hence my tears. I said I didn't know why I was crying and he said sometimes that's just what can happen and you wake up feeling groggy. I felt surprisingly well the rest of the day; nothing like last time having IVF in the UK. I was up and about and eating lunch at the hotel via room service and then managed dinner downstairs. We even went to the supermarket. We got wonderful news; there were six good quality eggs. We were very happy and excited! I found it hard to believe that after being on a higher dose we had fewer eggs than last time; it seemed my left ovary didn't want to produce many eggs. That evening we watched the movie *San Andreas* on the iPad and packed our bags.

Sunday – Today we moved hotels to be relaxed by the sea in 5-star luxury. We were really looking forward to this move. We tried to stop by the metro mall en route but the shops were shut early. It was nice and sunny as we arrived at the Astir Palace. We got a lovely grand deluxe room with a large balcony and admired the view of the private marina and gardens. We went for a walk to the marina; there were a lot of huge yachts in, quite a sight. In the evening we ate dinner in the hotel and got talking to a nice waiter, who told us of all the famous people he had met who had stayed at the hotel. After dinner we listened to a pianist play and drank a toast to our embryo transfer the next day.

Monday – Embryo transfer day. Finally! It felt like it had been a long trip so far but here we were, finally, at the pinnacle moment. I was sedated and given Intralipids again

The Infertility Crossroads

for the transfer. We had three embryos transferred. Two were of good quality and one was not so good, but they said it was still worth transferring. We were very excited: surely out of the three one would work? Or maybe I could end up with triplets! It had been a long time coming, but it was worth the wait. I had to pick up medicine afterwards at the local pharmacy to support the embryos; I would be taking three different types: two tablets and one in pessary form. I went back to the hotel and watched *the Minions* to relax. We both felt happy and relaxed; now we had a long wait (two weeks) in front of us.

Tuesday – I woke up with heartburn, maybe a good sign? It was our last full day in Greece. We ate breakfast outside on the terrace and admired the view. We took a golf buggy to the beach club. It was sunny but a little breezy. We walked back for lunch and then I took a nap. In the afternoon we walked around the sports club and had a look at the neighbouring hotel, the Westin, which is part of the same hotel chain. I remember seeing wild cats and tortoises that evening. The cats were checking the hotel out for food. We enjoyed the perks of the free snacks and drinks on the fourth-floor lounge of the hotel.

Wednesday – Finally the trip had come to an end and we were off home. We were looking forward to going home and feeling really positive and happy: we had our three embryos on board. I was trying to stay really relaxed and positive. I really thought, and so did Mark and my mum, that the IVF was working. By day five I had to go out and buy a new bra because mine simply didn't fit anymore. Now that didn't happen in the last round of IVF. By day nine I started to feel unwell, and in the evening I had a temperature and high blood pressure. I thought I didn't want anything to compromise my embryos so maybe I needed some antibiotics; I took a trip to the local A&E. They kept me in for monitoring for ovarian hyperstimulation syndrome, just like the first time I did IVF. When I got put on a ward I was told to write down my fluids, in and out. I was feeling nauseous in the morning. The consultant came round to do her rounds and talked to me about monitoring; and right before she left she dropped the bombshell. 'We did your blood test and the pregnancy test came back negative. I'm sorry,' she said. Then she undid the curtains surrounding my bed; I was surrounded by three other women looking at me crying my eyes out. I felt very alone. I was absolutely devastated and shocked. I was shaking and crying. I really didn't want to be there. The women around me, who were there for different reasons, got out of their beds and came over to comfort me, hugging me and talking to me. It was one of the nicest acts of kindness I've experienced in my life. Especially given how abruptly and rudely the doctor announced the news. She didn't show any care in the way she said it; surely she could have asked if I wanted the curtains shut so I could grieve in privacy. These women made me feel better; I plucked up the courage to call my husband who, bless him, was driving the truck at work. Mark was devastated too; we both found it so hard to believe that it hadn't worked.

I didn't want to be at the hospital; I wanted to go home and grieve. I asked the nurses to discharge me; they were very reluctant to do it and they took ages to provide me with a discharge paper. An hour had passed and I was still waiting on paperwork, so I just got up and left, saying I'm sorry but I need to go. I got some evil looks off the nursing staff but I didn't care; none of them had been sensitive to my needs; I had to take care of myself. I went home and cried. Mark and I didn't believe that a blood test would have been that accurate on day ten, and I wasn't bleeding, so we had another blood test done, just in case it was wrong. I had to travel really far away to get the blood test done too. The next day I got the negative result, confirming IVF number 2 had failed. Shortly after I started to bleed and was in agony. It felt like I was having a mini miscarriage. It was horrible and we were both really upset.

The house was quiet, very quiet and sad.

7. Picking up the pieces, moving on with adoption and the cat who saved us

A few days later, at the end of April, we were going to fly to Edinburgh to visit friends and family, which was a good distraction for us.

We couldn't shake the feeling that the house was too quiet; it should have been filled with the excitement of a pregnancy, and instead there was nothing. Out of the blue I suggested to Mark that we go to an animal shelter and find out about adopting a cat and see if it was something we wanted to do. We had never owned a cat in our lives before but off we went, both unsure but looking forward to seeing all the animals.

Wow! There were lots of cats on both sides of what seemed like a long corridor, all in little boxed houses with a glass door and access to an outdoor pen. Through another door were the kittens, but we weren't interested in a kitten for fear it would ruin the furniture. We spoke to the care handler and she told us about lots of the cats individually and what they needed. Mark saw a white cat with black patches that appeared to paw at the glass door. He liked the look of her, but I was too busy looking at two cats who were housed together. Mark persuaded me that we shouldn't start with two cats as it might be hard work. I agreed and then we wondered how we could narrow this search down when they were all so cute. We told the woman we would choose a cat based on personality, as that seemed like the logical thing to do and one that would meet our needs. I told her I would like one that sits on our lap and liked a cuddle and one that wouldn't mind just the house and the garden. The woman narrowed it down to two cats: Fluffy, the white and black cat that Mark had his eye on, and another darker brown/black cat. Fluffy was still trying to get out of the box to see us by pawing the glass. The woman let Fluffy out of the box and she really liked us straight away, letting us pet her and rubbing her head on my hand. I came around to liking her a lot. We decided, though, that we would stick to our guns and go away and think about it and decide away from the animal shelter.

We went home and decided Fluffy was the one for us, albeit we would change her name. Fluffy was a ten-year-old cat and her owner had sadly passed away, so she needed re-homing. Fluffy had already lived at the animal shelter for two months, which seemed like a long time in such a small box; no wonder she was pawing to get out. We were told she was an indoor cat, which suited us. Not many people re-home the older cats, we were told, which seemed a shame. So we knew we were doing the right thing adopting her. It was our first taste of adoption and it felt good.

We reserved her with a view to collecting her after our trip to Edinburgh that weekend. We were both very excited! Just the idea of owning her brought us happiness. We had to have a home visit first just to check the house was suitable, which only took five minutes of our time.

Off to Edinburgh we went and at the airport we spoke on the phone with the consultant in Greece; he simply said we could try again and we had to really work to get him to answer our questions. We asked what grade our embryos were. He said that the better two were grade 2. Then the call literally ended. I looked at my phone and it said the call time was two minutes. I couldn't believe it. It felt like they had our money and now they weren't interested. I would have expected a more detailed conversation, without me having to probe him for answers; instead, whenever I wasn't talking he was just silent. We weren't impressed and decided we wouldn't go back to that clinic again, based on the doctor's lack of communication.

We enjoyed our weekend in Edinburgh, but couldn't help feeling the whole time we were just waiting to pick up Fluffy on the Tuesday; we were really excited about it. Tuesday soon came around and I went to collect her. She meowed the whole way home, unsure of where she was going and who I was. I just talked to her and I knew straight away she was going to be a talkative cat. She settled in really well and I took the week off to be with her at home. We had to get used to a cat being around. I kept expecting her to jump out and give me a fright; I wasn't used to having a cat roaming around the house. At first we put a collar on her with a bell so we could sense where she was in the house, but that soon became annoying and actually she just fitted in and we got used to her presence. We renamed her Eva after our friend in Florida, one of the nicest ladies we've ever met, and also after the Disney movie *wall-e*, where wall-e would say 'Eeevaaa' ever so cutely to the white robot, Eve.

Eva was wonderful; she would greet Mark in the evening when he came in from work and do tricks for treats. She'd even sit by the treat cupboard expecting to do the routine for treats. She would sit on our laps and watch TV with us. The bay window brought her endless joy watching the locals walking the dogs. We nicknamed it her 'cat TV'.

I developed a real sense of responsibility for her; she was like my baby. She cuddled me in bed in the morning and purred away. When I was sad and cried she would comfort me. When I was ill she would sit by me. I honestly can't stress enough how therapeutic she was for us at this difficult part of our lives. When I went through IVF, Eva would sit on my tummy specifically and keep it warm; it was like she knew! Mark got so much out of his relationship with Eva, and we felt very happy with her in our lives. I now know other people who have struggled with infertility and they also did the same, filling the house with animals to help ease the pain. I highly recommend getting a pet if you're in a low place; they really can make you feel happier.

As we had planned, after our second attempt at IVF failed, we pressed on with the adoption process. We both had to get time off work to go to the training sessions. The training took place over three days; two days the first week and one day the following week. It was a heavy schedule and quite draining, as there was so much to take in. People came in to talk to us, experts by experience: people who had adopted children, and people who had been adopted as children. The sessions covered many topics, such as why children are taken into care, the challenges prospective adopters may face, therapeutic parenting skills and why some children need this approach, letter box contact with the birth family, child development, how stress from the mother can affect the unborn baby. It all felt rather new but a lot of what was said seemed to be common sense. I knew a lot of this stuff already, from my job and having done research, but I did learn some interesting things. There was a social worker who sat in the corner and took notes on us, like the kinds of questions we asked and our how much we actively participated, so she could pass it on to our social worker. Of course they didn't announce this fact but it become obvious later in the process, when our social worker mentioned questions we had asked at the training sessions during home visits. To be quite honest, we felt that the effect of the training was largely negative; I don't know if they were just trying to scare off the people who weren't in it for the long haul, or they just didn't realise how much the focus was on the negative aspects, the challenges. There was a lot of stuff about the negative behaviour that the child might display. But the reality is you probably won't be presented with a child with every problem under the sun, so it really felt like there was a lot of irrelevant information to take in. We were aiming to take on a young baby, so it had as few memories of its past as possible, compared with an older child. Of course all adopted children have to face the loss of their parents and we were told that most children battle with control over their food, but we were trying to block all the negativity and just think of the normal day-to-day life with a child.

After we had finished the training we moved onto the next stage, which involved home visits to assess us as potential parents. This involved about ten visits, one a week, with the same social worker who had been assigned to assess us. She would then write a report on us which would go to the adoption panel; our social worker would represent us, presenting her recommendation for us.

We would often be set homework at the end of a session to complete for the next week. I was always keen to complete this straightaway. The visits were stressful; a constant probing at every detail of your life. They wanted to know about our upbringing, our fertility journey, our attitude towards adoption, our relationship with ex-partners, our relationship with family and our experience with children, even our love life. It really felt like a massive invasion of our private lives. We are private people and what really grated on us – and I mean really annoyed us – was that the same intrusive question would be asked perhaps ten times. This undermined our trust in our social worker; it felt like she didn't trust us, that she didn't believe us. Why ask the same question over and over again? I can understand asking twice for verification but it really felt as if the whole process was being dragged out. Our social worker was often inconsistent at keeping her word. Every week she said she would complete something on the adoption paper trail, but she would regularly leave it until the next week or the week after that. It got a bit tiring, especially as we would always keep our end of the deal and complete our homework on time. By July, our family visits were coming to an end and our social worker was supposed to start writing the report on us to take to panel. We were given a panel date for September to be approved as adopters.

8. Stress, illness, leaving work and renewing our vows

By August 2016, Mark and I were stressed and emotionally drained by our journey so far, and we knew that we were facing our last few months with the freedom that having no children brings, so I decided to book a cruise for us in September; I also wanted to renew our wedding vows, to create the wedding I had wanted originally, which would have been on a cruise ship with our friends and families, being married by the ship's captain. The reason we didn't do this the first time was that it would be incredibly expensive, and a lot to ask of our friends and family; plus it would have been a nightmare for everyone to get that much time off work all at the same time. Anyway, I was really excited about the cruise and renewing our vows. I went and bought a new wedding dress for the ceremony. I remember feeling like I really needed this holiday!

In August I started to feel unwell. I had lumps under my armpits and red spots. I felt tired and I went to the doctor, who was puzzled by my symptoms. She thought it was shingles, so she put me on shingles medication for two weeks. After a week I felt worse; I was sleeping fifteen hours a day and I was not getting better, just worse. I returned to the same doctor, who decided her first diagnosis must have been wrong, so she put me on an antibiotic. Just as I was getting better I got a cold virus for two weeks, which drained me even more. I felt as if all my energy, life and happiness were being sucked out from me as I struggled to cope with being ill for such a long time. I often found myself in tears at work as I watched the mothers in the park with their children, playing happy families. I so longed for that! I had to tell my employer how I was feeling and she was very supportive and would always find time to talk it through. But the whole experience left me in a vulnerable state.

The weather was excellent during the summer of 2016, so we spent a lot of time in the garden, lounging on the sun loungers, and we purchased an inflatable hot tub to relax in. However, we began to feel insecure about the whole adoption process as it got nearer to our date with the panel; we decided to have another go at researching IVF clinics in the UK and found a clinic in Wales with good reviews. My parents offered to fund a two-cycle IVF package. It just felt right at the time to try more IVF. I called the social worker to halt the adoption process and she was really surprised.

I was taking time off work because of illness and the day I was supposed to go back to work it all took a turn for the worse. One Monday at 2.30 am I woke up with a sudden sharp pain in my lower right abdomen. I tried to get up and walk the short distance to the en-suite bathroom, but I had to hold onto things to maintain my balance and I felt dizzy, like I could collapse at any moment; I was in agony. When I got back to bed I woke Mark up and told him to phone an ambulance. I was really scared; it felt like something had burst inside me. I had never felt the need to call an ambulance in my life before, but I was desperate for some help and to stop the pain so I didn't hesitate. Mark was really startled, having just woken up, but he was very good with me. Eva the cat came and sat by my side of the bed on the floor; she knew something was wrong. A paramedic car arrived, followed by an ambulance to take me to hospital. The paramedics kept me topped up on morphine and helped me down the stairs to the ambulance. I was shaking from the pain and having a panic attack at the same time; because of my fast breathing my face and hands started to go numb and tingly. I had to tell them my medical history. The paramedic in the ambulance was very sympathetic and nice to me. Mark drove to the hospital in the car and met me there. After much uncertainty from the doctors and many painful examinations, they suggested Pelvic Inflammatory Disease, which I knew wasn't the right diagnosis, and tests did not bear the diagnosis out. The other suggestion, from the ultrasound technician, was a burst cyst. They discharged me from hospital with a lot of antibiotic medication and no clear explanation.

I felt overwhelmed by illness and infertility stress. I knew I needed time to focus on my health and trying for a baby. I made the massive decision to leave work for six months and end my employment. Yes, I could have taken sick leave, but I'm not that type of person and I didn't know how long I would need. I also felt it wasn't fair to the children I had in my care; they needed continuity. It turned out to be the right decision, despite the financial stress that soon followed. If you are feeling overwhelmed and you can afford to take time out from work, I suggest you do take the time for yourself. When we are in a stressed state our health can take a hit and it can have a massive knock-on effect. Sometimes we need to just go back to the basics in life, getting up in the morning, eating at the right times in the day, taking naps, doing exercise, spending time with friends and family, without the world of work and the stress that it can often bring.

I ended up back in hospital a few days later, still tender in my lower body but with a new pain in my upper abdominal region. I was referred to the surgical team to rule out appendicitis. It took six days just to get a scan done. The hospital environment, the doctors scratching their heads, not seeing my husband much as he was working; it all made me feel isolated, almost institutionalised. I slept a lot, felt groggy from drugs and at night on came the excruciat-

The Infertility Crossroads

ing pain, which made me scream the ward down until they got it under control. Then when the doctors came to assess me in the morning they thought I was fine because they didn't see my episodes of pain at night. I was discharged with the problem still not diagnosed or resolved. I insisted I thought it was a stomach ulcer induced by all the antibiotics from the previous month, but apparently they didn't have the means to test for that while I was in hospital, as it is normally carried out in outpatients. A week after being admitted I left the hospital.

The cruise was wonderful, and gave us a real chance to recuperate. We were the happiest we had been in as long as I could remember. The day we renewed our vows was on our wedding anniversary, the 4th of September. We were at sea that day and the ceremony was beautiful, performed by the captain just as I had dreamed. We followed the ceremony with high tea in the main dining room and we were photographed at different locations around the ship. We got a lot of attention from the other cruise passengers. Overall it was a very special day, full of love and happiness. Feeling happy again was like a giant dose of the best medicine. Mark still talks about how wonderful that day was.

We cruised around the Mediterranean, and meanwhile I had to start my medication for the third round of IVF, which felt like an odd thing to be doing while we were still on the cruise. At the start of the holiday I wore a bikini and looked good and felt confident, but by the end of the two weeks I looked six months pregnant from all the bloating and water retention. Several fellow cruisers came up and congratulated us on our pregnancy. That was highly embarrassing, since there was no pregnancy, and it made me feel deeply upset; first, because I wished I was pregnant, and second because I wished I could look thin and healthy while I wasn't pregnant. One of the medications I took was testosterone gel rubbed on my legs. It was supposed to

The Infertility Crossroads

help with egg quality; but the main culprit of my large abdomen was the drug Norethisterone. I did reach out to the ship's doctor and I called my IVF clinic but there was nothing that could be done; I just had to grin and bear it. When we returned from our cruise our trips to Wales for IVF round 3 began.

9. IVF round 3 (clinic number 3)

We were now committed to our third round of IVF at a clinic in Wales. We chose this clinic because of its reasonable price, caring approach and the good reviews it received.

We chose a different approach for this round of IVF. We decided to use a different type of medication; something to stimulate my ovaries in hopes of a better response. So instead of Gonal F we used Fostimon and Menopur. For the pregnancy support, alongside the usual medication, I would also take baby Aspirin to thin the blood and help to feed the uterus with a good blood supply. At embryo transfer we used a new technique called 'embryo glue'; the adhesive effect of the medium was designed to help our embryos stick to my endometrium and aid implantation. I also went for an endometrial scratch before the process of egg collection; this is a procedure used to help embryos implant more successfully.

I had booked a scratch with sedation, because I was scared of the pain; but when I walked into the procedure room I quickly realised there was no anaesthetist. I felt as if I was bullied into having the procedure without the anaesthetic. I don't know their reasoning for being like that with me, considering I had already paid for the sedation. I hadn't anticipated this and it made me feel very vulnerable. I just shut down my emotions and sucked it up and let them do it, since I had travelled for three hours to get to the clinic. Looking back now, I realise I should have said something. No one should feel bullied into doing something they're not comfortable with.

The Infertility Crossroads

We then started the IVF protocol and Mark did all my injections for me while the clinic monitored my reaction to the follicle-stimulating drugs. It wasn't getting any easier having injections every day. When the day finally came for egg collection we drove down to Wales and I was put under sedation. Only this time it was very different. The sedation was not like the sedation I had in the previous two attempts. It was a different drug and I found the experience terrifying. I did not actually fall asleep until I was being wheeled back in my room when the procedure was over. I remember hearing the man saying, 'I'm putting the needle through your vagina now to collect the eggs'. Yes, I was getting pain medication, and I could see the man topping up the cannula in my arm with the medication (which made me feel spaced out) but I felt everything and I was so scared.

I didn't enjoy this experience one bit; I much preferred the earlier treatments, where I was put to sleep for the whole procedure. I was traumatised enough by going through everything to do with infertility; I didn't need one more bad memory. I highly recommend you check which drug your clinic uses if you're going for sedation. As far as I was concerned, the less I remembered about procedures the better. At the end of the day you have to feel good about your choices, and my choice was to remember as little of the painful stuff as possible.

The embryologist told us they had collected three eggs and the next day we were told all three had fertilised with ICSI. There were not enough eggs to attempt a half ICSI/half normal IVF for fertilisation, so we just had to go for ICSI; you might say we had to put all our eggs in one basket. The clinic made the decision to go for a day three transfer; the embryologist described the cell division as uneven, producing seven or nine cells instead of even numbers. I remember us both feeling disappointed. One blastocyst had stopped growing so we went for a double embryo transfer on day three. I remember eating pineapple, including the core, and avocados on this round, as it was meant to help with implantation and egg quality and improve our chances.

As per usual the two-week wait felt very long; but it was different this time. I of course was symptom spotting and comparing my progress to other women online. It drove me nuts but it's so hard not to compare. I had extreme nausea ten days after the transfer; I stayed up all night eating plain biscuits, trying to be sick or having diarrhoea. I thought for sure I was pregnant because I'd never experienced that before, but then I started spot bleeding and in came the negative thoughts. I was bleeding properly the day of my blood test but I went anyway; since I had had a double embryo transfer, perhaps one embryo had still implanted. I remember driving back from the blood test crying and in agony; I knew it was all over. My beta HCG blood test was negative and in flooded the sadness.

I'm convinced it must have worked to some degree this round, though, because I was so sick and once when I went to the bathroom I passed what looked like a miscarriage, a grey sac with a black dot in it.

I felt like we had lost hope in the IVF process and my body. We had another round booked with the clinic because it was cost-effective paying for two rounds, but this loss hit us hard and, what with all the health problems I'd been having, I was overwhelmed.

10. Hitting rock bottom, illness, surgery and facing the truth

A few days after the IVF failed I ended up in hospital again. The stomach pain was back with a vengeance. This time I went to a different hospital in the hopes they would provide better care than the previous one. I could not eat or drink without being in agony, so much so I was curled over in pain on the floor. I had to get my lovely neighbour to take me to hospital because my husband was at work. After all three IVFs with my own eggs I had ended up in hospital; this was a continuing trend. Of course as soon as I mentioned IVF to the doctors in A&E they sent me straight to the gynaecology ward, but I felt the problem was my stomach, not my reproductive system.

I ended up in hospital for another six days. I lost a lot of weight and ended up on a drip for fluids because I couldn't eat or drink. I lay in a more or less vegetative state, on painkillers, sleeping and barely functioning. It was horrendous! I barely saw my husband because he was working and no one else came to see me. I felt so alone, at my lowest point so far, and I seriously questioned what life was all about for me. My parents were in Florida and I'd lost touch with my friends. Why was I on this path, a path that felt like self-destruction?

The only thing that made me feel any better, surprisingly, were the lovely friends I made in my ward. There were six beds in the room, with some women coming and going from hospital during my stay. Two of the women shared their stories of miscarriage, which I witnessed them go through. We hugged and cried and it ended up being a really therapeutic place for me. I had time to reflect on our

The Infertility Crossroads

loss. I shared my sadness with others and they shared theirs with me. I have to say, a miscarriage ward has got to be one of the saddest places you can be, but here I was feeling supported by these strangers. If you are ever as unfortunate as I was to land yourself on a ward like that don't be afraid to reach out to the other women; chances are you are feeling the same and you can help each other heal.

My stomach issues never resolved fully during my six-day stay, but they did put me on the waiting list to get a camera down to my stomach to have a look for a possible ulcer or other causes. I managed to drink and eat plain foods like mashed potato by the time I left the hospital. I also had a scan while in hospital which showed I had a 3-4 cm endometrioma cyst on my ovary. Oh great, I thought, here we go again! Another reason to push for the laparoscopic surgery I had been waiting eleven months for, well over the official 18-week surgery waiting time. When I left the hospital I was put on tablets, to try and coat the lining of my stomach. It seemed to calm down and settle as the weeks went by.
Mark and I began to talk about IVF. We could see it ruining my body, my life and we had lost all hopes after our dismal (in our eyes) amount of eggs and poor egg quality. We asked the clinic for a refund for the fourth treatment round while we regrouped.

I continued to search for solutions to our infertility. I felt at my most hopeful and productive when doing so. By this point I had been scouring the internet for years for answers to our infertility, but this time I found something new; I came across a clinic in Athens, Greece, called Serum. They performed a test which was not carried out in the UK. It involves sending a sample of menstrual blood over for testing for hidden infections. There are two types of tests. The first one includes an 'ordinary' test for Chlamydia Trachomatis, a test of total bacterial load (which measures the level of 'good bacteria' (lactobacilli) – a reduced population tends to indicate an abnormal vaginal environment caused by another, more hostile, bacteria, such as E-coli, Proteus etc., Urea plasmas; two species of Mycoplasmas – Mycoplasma Genitalium and Mycoplasma Hominis; two other Bacterial Vaginosis species – Gardnerella Vaginalis and Atopobium Vaginae; and Herpes group viruses – HSV1, HSV2 and CMV; and HHV 6 (a virus recently linked to unexplained female infertility).

Then there is the second test for hidden Chlamydia called the Locus Medicus (LM) test.

I was told by the lovely Penny, the director at Serum, that one test may show hidden Chlamydia while the other may not, so it was best to have both tests done. The test was simple enough to carry out; I sent off my sample in a sterile container I got from my GP. The results came in and I was shocked. What I had heard was true; the NHS test for Chlamydia showed up negative in the UK for years, but when I was tested for this more chronic hidden strain of Chlamydia I tested positive. Now I know there is a stigma around sexually transmitted diseases but I am not afraid to talk about it. I don't want there to be any stigma attached. I wish these tests were available and supported in the UK. I probably have an ex-boyfriend, cheating on me, to thank for it but also there is the possibility that it came from a toilet seat, which I always thought was a myth until my gynaecologist confirmed there are many strains of the virus and it can be caught that way.

I also tested positive for HHV6 virus, which is linked to a childhood illness; in recent years studies have shown a correlation between carriers of this virus and infertility. I was put on a large course of antibiotics and antiviral drugs for a month and so was Mark. I felt extremely relieved that

I had had a further investigation that might clear up a problem; perhaps this would make a big difference to my infertility.

Along came Christmas and this year it felt really sad. Still no children in our lives, and then came the sad news that my Gran had passed away on the 21st of the month. I had a great connection with my Gran and I truly felt a loss with her passing. She was always wonderful with children and I always felt I inherited my love of children from her.

Between Christmas and New Year I decided I was so fed up of feeling in pain and waiting for the NHS to give me my operation I would call them and ask to speak to someone in management. Well I don't know how I or they did it but they found me an operation slot on Friday the 13th of January. Take it or leave it, they said. Yes you heard me right: Friday the 13th. That made me very nervous. I had no choice; I needed the operation and I couldn't afford it privately, so I accepted that date.

On the 31st of December my second nephew was born. I really struggled with my emotions throughout the announcement of my brother and sister-in-law's pregnancy, but there I was on the 31st of December; the first family member to visit him. Such a surreal moment for me, it reminded me of the heartache of my journey so far and the yearning for a family of my own. I could only show my happiness for them outwardly, and of course it was lovely holding my new nephew. When I looked at him I could see my brother and sister-in-law in his face. I knew the chances of me ever seeing a similar reflection of myself or my husband were looking slim.

It was time to move on, to a new year and a new unknown. The day finally came for the camera to look down my throat into my stomach, which I was so nervous about. The thought of gagging on a camera filled me with fear. I was feeling better now, and it had been two months since my stint in hospital.

The morning of the procedure I went to the hospital with my mum. I could see how nervous the other patients in the waiting room were too. I just reminded myself that it wouldn't last forever and told myself to be brave; after all, it's better to have it checked out and be sure there was nothing that needs attending to than not have the procedure. I had a light sedation in my arm, which I can tell you had no effect on me personally. There were lots of people in the room to keep me calm and hold me still. The consultant was an older gentleman with a calm and informative manner. I lay on my side and he kept talking to me throughout. I had an anaesthetic spray to numb my throat, which felt very weird and uncomfortable. That was followed by the very uncomfortable process of swallowing the camera; it made me gag a few times but nothing but air would come out. I relaxed on a beach in my mind as a distraction technique, as much as I could and, with the effects of the sedation I tried to remain still and I remember it would be soon over. I was so relieved when they finished! That is an understatement. I felt super brave! The report was all clear and I was given a clean bill of health for my stomach, which, to be honest, I wasn't surprised about, given it was now a couple of months later.

In January we held the funeral for my Gran. It was a beautiful ceremony and I'm sure it was just what my Gran would have loved. The week of my Gran's funeral was a tough week for me; I had the funeral mid-week and my operation on the Friday, to remove any endometriosis or anything else they would find.

The day of my operation I was nervous. There were two things I was particularly nervous about. The first was the scarring on my abdomen from the surgery; the cuts, which filled me with dread of ever wearing a bikini again. The other thing was the thought of being filled with gas so they could carry out the operation. It would expand the cavity enough so they could carry out the procedure. The surgeon reassured that me the cuts would only be around 1cm long. I would have one in my navel and two in my abdomen.

My operation was scheduled for lunchtime and I was starving, having not been allowed food. My husband, mum and I sat in the waiting room and then a NHS member of staff came out and told everyone waiting for surgery there were no more free beds in the hospital, so they were waiting for beds. This meant some of the surgeries would have to be cancelled. Then the TV in the waiting room, broadcasting the news, told us exactly the same story. The NHS was struggling to free up beds and therefore cancelling operations. After a long delay I was called through for surgery, which I was told I was very lucky to be having; they said I would be the only gynaecology case seen that day. I felt relieved; I just wanted it over and done with. I don't think they would have dared to cancel my surgery, given I had waited exactly a year!

If you find yourself facing surgery for the first time please don't fear it. The anaesthetists are trained to put you at ease. This is how I coped with going under a general anaesthetic. I told myself I trust my surgeon and the team looking after me. I put myself on a beach in my mind, as that was a relaxing place to be, and when the oxygen mask was placed over my face I stayed on the beach in my mind and told myself I would keep my eyes open as long as possible, until they closed for me. When I woke up it felt like five minutes later. The reality was I had been in surgery for an hour and a half and recovery for a further half an hour.

The Infertility Crossroads

Two nurses were standing either side of me, trying to make me comfortable. I was shaking and in pain. They sorted that out with pain medication and blankets. I remember one nurse telling me I wasn't very well in recovery and my surgery had taken longer than expected. While I was in the recovery bay an assistant surgeon I had not met before came by and told me they had drained the cyst and that I had areas of endometriosis dotted around on my pelvic area and bowel (which they were unable to remove because they would need a bowel surgeon and it was risky surgery). My ovary was stuck to my uterus. My uterus was stuck to my pelvic wall. The dye test showed a blocked fallopian tube. I had moderate endometriosis. I was overwhelmed with information and half asleep from surgery. The nurses then disappeared and I was eventually transferred to a ward. I am able to write this information now, but I can tell you that at the time what I was told was too brief and soon forgotten in my daze from being under general anaesthetic. I was met by my mum and husband, as I was wheeled into the ward. They looked really relieved to see me and I reassured them I was ok, but of course told them the story of how I had not been well. They told me they hadn't expected me to be so long in surgery either, but that they had kept themselves busy while they were waiting.

I had a bit of a relapse when I arrived at the ward. I was bleeding a lot and I was in a lot of pain and felt generally unwell and couldn't compose myself. The nurses had to lift me to clean me and made me more comfortable with morphine. Mark was very good with me and he stayed with me until 10 pm, as we were told the surgeon would come and see us to discuss the surgery. I wasn't well enough to go home, so what was meant to be day surgery turned into an overnight stay. It was the best place for me, though. My mum left the hospital around dinner time. Mark and I were very disappointed when the surgeon didn't show up to discuss my surgery that night, and Mark left to go home. I

The Infertility Crossroads

was sad to see him leave, when I really wanted him to stay and take care of me.

The next morning I was still in pain and on morphine. I remember the nurses arguing about me going home. One nurse said I could go home with morphine in hand and the other nurse said, well, if she's in that much pain and on morphine she's not well enough to go home. Anyway the decision was made; they needed the bed for other patients and I was sent home.

I rested at home while Mark was at work and then came the most excruciating pain ever! I remember I wanted to go to bed early so I got in my pyjamas and went to lie down on the bed. As I lowered my upper body onto the bed the most excruciating pain went through my upper body, all the way to my shoulder tip. I screamed out in pain. I began to panic; every little movement meant the pain ripped through me, getting worse, and it was already 10/10 pain. I was alone in the house, screaming. I grabbed my phone and screamed hysterically and cried down the phone to my parents, asking for help. My mum answered the phone and her immediate reaction, not being able to make out the words I was saying, was to think something had happened to our cat. She eventually understood that I was in great pain and told me she would be right over to the house to take me to the hospital. In the meantime she called my neighbour, who was a nurse, to come and see me, and she arrived with her husband. I was so embarrassed, I was standing in my pyjamas, screaming in pain and crying, but I was so grateful for their company. Our neighbour tried to help and calm me down. She knew it was the gas they had used during the operation; it had travelled to my shoulder tip and was causing the excruciating pain. I wished I had never left the hospital. I was really glad to go back there. I had to wait for hours in A&E to be seen. When the doctors saw me they told me there was

The Infertility Crossroads

nothing that could be done except to control the pain and wait for the gas to leave my body naturally. Looking back now at the operation, I can tell you that the laparoscopy was a breeze; the difficult bit was the gas pain.

After a few days things calmed down. I stood in front of the mirror and watched my inflated, swollen belly calm down. I tended to my stitches, keeping them clean and well dressed; eventually, after a couple of weeks, I took them out myself. It didn't hurt but I felt better about taking them out; there was no way they were ever going to dissolve themselves and I didn't want my scars to heal strangely or get infected. The scars were small and I accepted that in a year's time they would fade and it would have been worth it. I do recommend to anyone having surgical laparoscopy to get your stitches checked to see if you need them taken out; they normally send you home after the operation with no follow-up for weeks. I think a little bit of extra TLC goes a long way.

Following my surgery, Mark and I were feeling overwhelmed with everything my body had been through and, although the money was there for another round of IVF, we were feeling doubtful that it would lead to a successful pregnancy.

11. Starting a petition

At the start of the year 2017, although we felt we had moved on from IVF, I decided to do something positive, to try to promote change in the NHS system, or at least do something to contribute to a debate in the NHS. You see, there is a postcode lottery around which IVF treatment is available. Each CCG decides how much funding they put into IVF and that varies between each CCG.

I write this in 2018, in hopes that by the time you are reading this book things have changed for the better. The area in England where I live provides one free round of IVF on the NHS; but if I still lived in Scotland, where I grew up and lived nineteen years of my life, I would have received three free attempts. The NICE guidelines recommend three attempts should be provided to infertile couples. As well as the postcode lottery, another challenge between CCG groups is the additional criteria which affect women and make them exempt from free treatment. For example: age, healthy weight, not having children from a current or previous relationship. I believe we should all be equal no matter where we live, our postcode, our circumstances or age.

I was invited to parliament at the time to support a debate going on around IVF and the NHS, but unfortunately I could not attend; but at least my petition was supporting the issue.

It would mean a lot to me if you could sign my petition. This petition needs every signature and bit of support it can get. Here is the website address for you to add your signature. Feel free to add a personal comment or note to me.

https://www.change.org/p/jeremy-hunt-fund-ivf-consistently-for-all-not-via-a-postcode-lottery

12. Restarting the adoption process and adoption breakdown

We had pretty much given up on IVF, when we received a letter from the adoption agency reminding us our application would expire soon if we did not return to it. We felt we had put so much effort into the adoption process so far that it would be wrong for us to not continue and try to adopt a child. We felt that the world war with my body was over and we accepted that adoption would be right for us.

I went to my doctor and decided to have the Depo Provera shot, which would give me a break for three months from my periods. My periods were a constant reminder of us failing to conceive each month, and I just wanted them to stop so I could be in peace.

Once we made the decision to continue with adoption we called the social worker and she came back out to see us at home. We had to restart the home visits. Once a week the social worker would come out and extract every bit of information about our lives, relationships, infertility and childhood. What support network would we have going forward in the adoption process and what kind of child did we have in mind to adopt? She seemed to probe even deeper than before. She questioned our medical records, and we had to pay for our records to be updated at the GP surgery. This led to things we didn't even know had been written about us, including some factually incorrect statements, which led to us to having to defend ourselves and the truth of our medical history. Imagine trying to tell the truth versus a doctor's word. It made us look like we were lying. It frustrated us no end. I had phone calls late at night from social workers asking the same question for the tenth time. Maybe they thought we would change our answers. I thought the whole thing was rather strange; I knew they were there to test us and put us through the wringer, so to speak. Were we good enough in the agency's eyes? We kept asking ourselves why it felt like such an uphill battle.

Our social worker never completed her paperwork on time and right before we got to panel she still hadn't written our report.

Then one night I received a phone call from the adoption team to tell me there had been multiple adoption breakdowns, and couples losing their trust in the adoption agency. This worried us. Why were other couples feeling the same as us? Something just didn't feel right. Surely, it wasn't meant to be this hard? We thought about moving to a different agency, one that we felt would work with us, but in reality that wasn't going to work out; our agency was merging with all the local agencies, creating one super group, so chances were, we would have been right back at square one, dealing with the same people.

We felt that to move forward, we would have to change to a supportive agency; we just didn't feel that this agency was the one. We felt the agency didn't like our infertility story and perhaps they preferred older couples who had already had their own children. We sadly made the decision to stop the adoption process. The process we had spent another six months on, a year and a half in total from when we first started.

We felt very angry for a couple of months and that led to sadness and emptiness. As a couple we became bitter about the adoption process. We would have given an adopted child a wonderful home and life with two loving parents. I know people who have had both good and bad experiences with adoption and I highly recommend that, if you choose this route, you choose an agency based on a personal recommendation from someone who has adopted through them. You also need a thick skin and a willingness to persevere.

Before approaching any adoption agency, gain the support of your family and friends. Read as many adoption books as possible and look at adoption videos or footage on YouTube. You will be asked about all this in the adoption process. If you are going down this road I say this from my heart: I truly hope you succeed. It is a wonderful thing you are doing. I only wish that we had had the good fortune – and the strength – to get to the end.

13. Finding myself again (weight loss, friends & something to look forward to)

I had to lift this dark cloud that was looming over my head and raining tears on me. I literally couldn't see the sun. Every morning I would wake up, check-in with myself: 'What am I doing today? How am I feeling today? What's just happened in my life?' The last part especially would get me every time. The mirror, of all items in my house, was honestly what helped me through these dark times. I hated my reflection half the time and the woman who looked back was nothing like before; I had water retention, bloating, extra fat on my body, new scars, spots from hormones, dry scalp, oily hair, dry skin. I was far from the woman I used to be, but the mirror was a path to self-motivation, as I could literally reflect on myself.

The Depo Provera shot, which was supposed to give me a break for three months from my periods, was doing the complete opposite. It made me bleed every day. It ruined my day, ruined my love life, and made me dizzy and anxious. Sometimes I would look myself in the eyes in the mirror and cry, talking to myself in my mind, either angry – 'Why me?' or trying to calm myself down – 'There's always someone more worse off than you, Heather! So don't be sad!' I got to the point where I would tell myself, 'You are strong! You are strong!'

I got my body back in shape by joining a gym and working with a few different personal trainers. The personal trainer (Tracy McLaren) I have ended up working with to this day is one of the most amazing women. I've ever met. She smiles constantly, listens extremely well and pushes you when you need pushing in order to achieve results. Going to a personal trainer was like therapy for me. I honestly think that women going through infertility should all have personal trainers. If the NHS could prescribe personal trainers we'd all be so much more positive! I think it's like the secret answer to lots of side-effects related to infertility; it just makes you feel so good about yourself, stronger and more confident when confidence is at an all-time low. It's money well spent! Especially if you get a female trainer who understands the womanly side of things.

I made an effort to make friends and socialise. I felt some of my friends had grown distant and some had even left my side. I felt isolated. Perhaps they couldn't relate to my own problems, they didn't know what to say? I mean I must have been bad company, always talking about negative subjects like loss and heartache. I learnt over the years that, in order to maintain friendships, I had to show two sides. Yes, share the vulnerable side and the struggles we were going through as a couple; but then talk about other, more positive things in my life or the world, because otherwise I wasn't much company and chances were my friends wouldn't want to meet up as much.

I needed, we needed, something to look forward too. So we had some adventures on some fantastic holidays! I mean, really, we had a great time, but I can tell you, personally; it didn't matter if I was halfway around the world, there were always those quiet moments were I was sad we didn't have a family. I think that just comes with the nature of infertility, it follows you wherever you are; it will always be a small part of you. You just have to accept that it's ok to feel that way, and take some of the weight off your shoulders. It is okay to feel whatever you want to feel; you have to go through the emotions. For me the emotion of emptiness, childlessness, with me wherever I was in the world, led me straight back to the world of IVF.

14. The sudden loss of Eva

On the 17th of May 2017 I got up for work for what I thought would be a normal day. I noticed that Eva didn't wake me up at 4 am with her usual meowing and I searched the house for her, to greet her. I looked in every room twice until eventually I found her behind the open door in the spare bedroom. There was only a small gap between the open door and the wall where she sat. I knelt down to pet her and she immediately began to purr, but she had her head down. I thought she must be tired so I went downstairs and made my breakfast, but she didn't follow me as usual. When I was ready for work I said goodbye and off I went.

When I was at work I had a strange feeling about Eva. I texted Mark and told him she was behind the door and don't open the door further and knock her. I didn't hear back so I thought I'd better phone him and tell him to check on her; he thought she was ok. Later that morning I got a panicked phone call from Mark saying Eva was ill, she'd done a wee on the mat, which she had never done before, and then he said her legs sort of gave way and she was struggling to breathe, and he was taking her to the vets. I told him to take her straight there and I would take the girl I was looking after and meet him there. Mark told me that by the time he got to the vets her tongue was hanging out and she was gasping for breath. She was put on oxygen straight away. The vet later came out and told us she thought Eva was having an asthma-like allergic reaction and her lungs had fluid in them. They would treat her with steroids and a diuretic; it was not safe to sedate her to drain the fluid manually because of how unstable her breathing was. We were both really worried about her.

Mark had to rush off to work and I sat with the little girl, waiting to see how things went. The little girl was very happy in the vet's waiting room and cheered me up, as much as one could cheer up in this terrible situation. The vet later came back out to speak to me and said she would ring at the end of the day to let me know how things were going; Eva would stay at the vets overnight and we'd see how things were in the morning. The vet was smiling so I felt more hopeful and calmer. So off I went to the town centre with the little girl to a coffee shop to calm myself and eat some sugar; my heart felt like it was racing. At the coffee shop the girl continued to cheer me up with her caring gestures. It was like she knew. We then went to the library and back to the car park to head home. Just as I was driving off I got a call from Mark, his voice frantic, saying, 'Eva's not doing well, she's really not doing well'. I needed to go back to be with her. My heart sank! I pulled the car over and rang the little girl's parents and told them the situation and said I'd need to drop her off back into their care. Luckily, I was right by her mother's workplace so I raced round and dropped her off then sped off to the vets.

Once I got to the vets the vet invited me through the back. At that point I got scared; I thought she was calling me somewhere private to tell me Eva had died, but I was wrong. Eva was in the back room in an oxygen box. She was gasping for air and looking towards the black side wall of the box. I tapped on the glass to see if she would turn her head towards me but she was so busy concentrating on breathing. Eventually she turned her head a bit. I was crying and I spoke softly to her. I couldn't believe it; this was the first time I had seen her since she had been at the vet.

The vet explained she wasn't responding to treatment and every time they tried to move her for a scan she would go blue, unable to breathe so they couldn't scan her. They had done an x-ray and they had sent it to another vet's practice for a referral opinion. They told me to head home and wait for a call once they had word from the other vet's practice. I got in the car and cried all the way, until I was nearly home and then the phone rang again. It was the vet. I pulled the car over and once again my heart sank and I thought they were going to tell me she had died. Well, it was pretty much the worst news I could possibly hear except for that. She was still alive but the prognosis from the other vet was she had cancer of the liver on both sides and it would be inoperable. The vet went on to talk a whole load of medical terms about her lungs and breathing which all became a blur in my mind, then it was followed by the words, 'the kindest thing to do is put her to sleep'. She was going to die and it was not fair to let her struggle anymore; she was stressed and exhausted from gasping for breath and the medicine wasn't working. The vet asked me to come back. I told her to wait and I rushed back to the vets to be by her side. I called Mark on the way and he was devastated. He shouted down the phone, 'Why has she got cancer!' He just couldn't believe it. Our luck had once more turned for the worse. 'Come on, what else are you going to hit us with in this life? We can't take anymore!' I thought.

When I got there she was not in the oxygen box anymore, she was on the vet's table with an oxygen mask being held to her mouth. The vet gave me a stool to sit beside her. I stroked her head and spoke to her softly while crying my eyes out. Eva turned to me and when she saw me she tried to jump into my arms, which immediately made her very distressed with her breathing and made her bark like a dog, which was the noise of the fluid in her lungs. The nurse reached forward to grab her and calm her and asked her to lie back on the table so she could breathe again, which Eva did. What a good girl, listening to the nurse, I thought. However, I was horrified by what I had just witnessed. The desperation in Eva's face and body. The pain and suffering was too much to bear. 'Please just do it now, put her to sleep, out of her pain.' I stroked her head and the vet asked once more if she could give her the injection. I agreed, crying my eyes out. It was so peaceful. I stroked her and I said, 'Eva we love you, we love you', as she went to sleep. Her eyes became lifeless as she died but she was still so beautiful.

Eva passed away at 2 pm. The vet asked if I wanted a minute with her and I sat there crying, stroking her and talking to her. Then I called Mark and confirmed she had passed. Mark agreed I would take her to the crematorium, as he didn't want her to go to the incinerator with other animals. I agreed. After the call I realised I didn't have enough charge in my electric car to get there because it was really far away; I rang the lovely lady who had looked after Eva a few weeks ago when we were on holiday and she immediately said, 'I'll be there in fifteeen minutes to take you'. We both went on a long expedition to find this place, which was an hour away, the last bit down a mile-long farm track, extremely bumpy, with Eva in the boot of the car in a cardboard coffin.

An old man kindly greeted us and I filled the form out and placed the box with Eva on the table and I said my goodbyes. I was exhausted and by the time I got home I went into my bedroom and sobbed my eyes and heart out! Poor Mark was at work and dealing with his grief alone. I texted my friend to tell her what had happened and that I couldn't bear being in the house with Eva's things everywhere. I couldn't help but keep looking for her in the house, even though she wasn't there. My friend invited me round and I spent the evening in her company sharing stories, and it really helped me. She me about her grief over losing a pet that was also her fertility companion and had been there for her through it all. I couldn't believe the same kind of thing had happened to her too.

I spent the next few days crying and longing for Eva. I felt a bit better when two days later I got Eva's ashes back, in a lovely oak casket with engraving on it: 'Eva'. Finally she was home. I put her in front of a framed photo of her next to the sofa she used to sleep on. We cleared the house of her things and then put her collars and mementoes in boxes I bought especially in memory of her. I ordered a photo book I made using Apple software and I ordered an engraved bracelet with 'Eva', a heart sign and a paw print on it. I recommend this as a nice gesture if you ever are unfortunate enough to lose a beloved pet; it really helped me.

Eva was so beautiful, intelligent, caring, loving, funny, playful and cute. What she gave us was extreme happiness! We actually would say aloud every day that we loved her and that she made us so happy. She would sleep by my side, follow me around the house like a shadow, sit on my lap at all times of the day, play with us and let us know when things weren't right because she was so intelligent. Like the time we left the freezer door open and she meowed constantly until we closed it, or the time she woke us in the night because someone was trying to break into Mark's car. It was definitely better to have loved and lost than to have never loved at all. I highly recommend getting a cat if you are going through infertility struggles or just have stress in your life. Eva was so therapeutic for us. Just talking to her, having her company and stroking her relieved stress. We always said she saved us, after coming back from Athens and the house being so quiet, sad and empty. Getting Eva was the best thing we ever did. Now, looking at it from a different perspective, I think we also saved Eva; she must have had that cancer a long time, perhaps before we got her and we gave her a great life up until that eventful last day. Eva was our nanny, she looked after us.

We went on to adopt another cat, called Skye, and then a friend for her a few months later, called Luna. I kind of think they were made to be together. Both one year old when we adopted them individually, their names just seemed to say they were meant to be with each other. They are good friends now and as my cat sitter calls them, they are 'my girls'.

15. Surgery number 2

After the laparoscopy surgery in January I felt better for about a month; then I started to become tired in the daytime. I kept mentioning it to my doctor who, at the start of the year, said, 'don't worry; we will get you pregnant this year'. I was told to relax, stop stressing, try yoga. I then began to get pain in my pelvic region and pain down my leg. The pain was worst when I was sitting. At night, trying to get to sleep was difficult. It was scary how much it was ruining my life. I became a shell of myself and lost confidence; the doctor wasn't listening to me and I felt she was implying that I was making the whole thing up. I would cry when she gave me her insensitive advice; she put me down and I didn't have the courage to push her for a second opinion or challenge her. No patient should feel this way. Don't ever let your gut instincts be squashed by a doctor! Keep persevering until someone listens to you.

I had just made a new friend that summer who told me she had had endometriosis and multiple surgeries in her life so far. Could I have endometriosis again? It was lucky for me that I met this woman as she passed on the details of her consultant, who she described as excellent. I contacted his secretary and arranged a private appointment within the week. My friend told me I could pay to see him privately and then if I wanted to wait, I could ask to be transferred onto his NHS list, or I could pay privately for an operation.

I went to the consultation on my own; he seemed like a pleasant man. In my mind I was expecting a scan when I got there but we talked and he asked how I would like him to help me. I told him my story and he suggested another laparoscopy just like that. 'When would you like it?' He asked. Again, just like that, so different from the NHS; you could snap your fingers and have the operation that week if you wanted. I told him I'd think about it. We also discussed having a hysteroscopy done at the same time. This meant inserting a camera in my uterus to look for any problems and a repeat of the dye test in the fallopian tubes to rule out other problems. I was at the point of pain and misery where I didn't care if I put the whole operation on credit cards or loans; I was having that operation and getting my life back. My kind parents stepped in once again and offered to pay for the procedure. They too wanted to see their daughter get her life back. I was so glad, grateful and relieved. It took the pressure off. I should have arranged the procedure immediately but I wanted to be courteous to the family I worked for as a nanny, so I arranged it to coincide with one week of their holiday. I knew I would need at least two weeks to recover, though, after my last experience.

It seemed like a long few weeks' wait, but the day finally arrived. I'd had my pre-op tests done and I was ready to get this over and done with again. I still couldn't believe it had only been six months since my last surgery for this horrible condition, endometriosis. I've been told by doctors that some people get endometriosis really bad and others don't even know they have it. Amazing how there can be such a contrast.

The morning of the surgery my husband took me to the private BMI hospital. I was warmly welcomed by all members of staff, even the cup of tea lady, as I like to refer to her. All I had to do was press my buzzer and she would cater to my food and drink requirements. There was a menu so I could pre-order food in my room. The room itself was very nice. It even had a sofa bed, which poor Mark immediately slumped on. He was very tired and I don't think he was handling it very well, that I was going for another operation, this time with my parents out of the country and not back from Florida until later that day. I felt a bit unsupported by my crashed-out husband, but looking back it was clearly just that he was dealing with all of this fear in his head for me.

I met with my consultant and we went through the surgery plan. I went down for surgery mid-morning and I felt calm and reassured in their care. When I woke in the recovery room I was surprised to see a tube coming out of my abdomen; I was told it was in place to drain excess blood. That meant I now had an additional incision. So one on the pubic bone area; one through the navel like last time; one through an old incision on the left and this new one on the right with the draining tube. Ok, so now in addition to one of the original scars I had five scars in total. Although they were small this did make me sad. Fair enough if I had a baby to show for these scars, but all I had was pain and experience. Call me vain, but I preferred my old body without the scars. I hoped my husband still liked the look of me; which of course he reassures me to this day he does. I was given more pain relief and taken back up to my room to be with my husband.

I was in pain trying to move or even get to a sitting position on the side of the bed to try to walk to the toilet. I was initially helped a lot. I struggled to pass urine, so the attentive nurses brought a scan machine to check for urine in my bladder. It turned out I was just really dehydrated from the surgery; my body had just absorbed all the liquid I had been drinking as it needed it. Later that evening I was fine. The cup of tea lady said I needed to drink lots of peppermint tea, which normally I wouldn't drink or hadn't thought of, but I took the suggestion on board and drank cup after cup; it really helped with all the gas put in my body during the operation. If only I had known this the

The Infertility Crossroads

last time I wouldn't have been in such agony. The gas pain this time was sore but nowhere near the 10/10 – let's scream the house down – pain of the last time. My pain was managed by peppermint tea and pain meds. A night stay in hospital was all part of the private treatment and much needed, I felt. Why the NHS doesn't do this as standard is beyond me. I was a lot happier. Mark left in the evening and the next day my parents, just back from Florida, came to get me. They had fruit pastilles in hand because I told them my mouth was really dry from the operation and nothing was working to help that. Gosh, those fruit pastilles tasted great and did the trick! I was really happy to see my parents; they greeted me with big hugs and smiles. There is nothing quite like your parents when you are ill. My consultant came by my room and spoke to my parents and me about the operation in great detail and showed me pictures. He told me the uterus looked good; the endometrioma (chocolate cyst) he had found was removed by excision of the cyst rather than draining, which he said would have meant the cyst would reform. He also removed scarring from the previous operation and took a biopsy from my uterus. Miraculously, and the best bit of news, was my fallopian tubes were both open and unblocked. I couldn't understand how this could be, considering the bad news I had received after the last laparoscopy, but he just said perhaps they were in spasm last time. In the photos I could see the dye coming out and proof of them working. I was happy that it was all looking good now and he just wanted to see me walk up and down the corridor to make sure that I was back on my feet properly. I was being discharged from the hospital and just needed the drain to be taken out of my abdomen by the nurse.

Getting the drain out of my abdomen was horrible. I thought the tube was only in a tiny bit, but the nurse kept pulling and pulling; it must have been on the other side of my abdomen internally. I screamed and my Dad heard me from the corridor. It felt like something moving inside of me and as it left the space it was once in, it hurt because the area inside was so tender. The nurse never put a stitch in, just covered it with a bandage and I thought, 'how's this going to heal properly?' but she reassured me it would just close and heal. A few days later I went to the local hospital and asked for the hole to be stitched with paper stitches. I didn't believe it would heal smoothly without them. The nurse did a great job with the paper stitches and smoothed it out so as to minimise the scar. The paper stitches were the last that I removed because I wanted the scar to heal nicely. I had my other stitches removed at my doctor's surgery by the nurse because I struggled this time; the stitches were made from a different material and tied more closely to the skin. It didn't hurt getting them out.

I had my follow-up consultation at the hospital and I was told the biopsy looked good; he gave me the pictures from my operation to keep and gave me a 20 percent chance of the endometriosis coming back, which I felt was ok odds. He told me he suspected that I had Adenomyosis; the only way to actually confirm the diagnosis is analysis after a hysterectomy, so we had to rely on guesswork for now. Adenomyosis is a condition in which the inner lining of the uterus (the endometrium) breaks through the muscle wall of the uterus. It had caused my menstrual cramps, lower abdominal pressure, and bloating before periods and I suspect it gave me heavy periods.

There was a lady in her 60s having endometriosis surgery the same day as me, and my consultant told me she had travelled from the other end of the country to have the operation. She was one of the unlucky ones; she had already had multiple surgeries and a hysterectomy but the endometriosis kept appearing in her body.

The Infertility Crossroads

I really hoped this was the end of my endometriosis surgery and in comparison to last time this surgery was a more positive experience. I wished I had kept my private medical insurance, so that it would have covered my surgery, but I had cancelled it a while back thinking I would never need it. In hindsight I should have kept it because I needed it. So after my surgery I found a very specific policy on the market called a fixed moratorium, which would now cover me, after two years, for this condition and pay for any future operations, should I need them. Even if I had symptoms or sought help within the two years it would not restart the clock, so to speak, like other policies. Exactly two years after my surgery I would be covered on the policy once again and I highly recommend this to everyone; when you are in pain you don't want to wait for months or fork out thousands, you want to be able to get the care you need fast. Of course I am covered for all other eventualities straight away.

16. IVF round 4 and 5 with Donor egg and surgery number 3

The adoption process had ended in the summer and once again the dark cloud rolled over our heads. This time it turned into anger. We both felt angry at how we had been treated; we bickered with each other over how it had ended and how we felt about our future. We missed Eva still, even though we had these new cats. The new cats required constant monitoring at first to make sure they got on. Then the household started to relax and so did the cats.

I felt like I was stuck in a rut. I needed a holiday desperately, to lift the dark cloud, so I begged Mark for weeks until finally he phoned me one day when he was at work and said, 'Ok, let's go to Florida'. Hooray!

We booked it for the following month and I was so excited. We were going with my parents too, so we could all spend time together in the Orlando and Sarasota areas.

As we were preparing for Florida the IVF conversation came up again. We both knew in our hearts we had to go down the route of donor eggs to have a shot of having a baby. We had been discussing this on and off for years, since it was first mentioned to us. It had never sat right with us before, particularly me, because I was the one losing out on a genetic tie to my child. However, once the adoption was off the cards, I was completely backed into a corner; this was my only chance for success, so I did a complete U-turn on the idea. I shocked myself. For some reason something lifted the dark cloud off the idea and told me to go for it. So I learned to let go and I say it again, I really did surprise myself that I accepted the idea. I

The Infertility Crossroads

embraced the idea that I could still carry my baby, and I wouldn't pass on my genetic infertility issues. I would still carry my husband's genes and recently in the news it was reported that the mother still passes on some of her DNA to the baby. I'm not saying I was 100 percent set on the idea but I was 95 percent comfortable with it, and that was enough for me to say: okay let's do it.

First of all, I went for a scan at a clinic locally; my mum came with me because I was concerned I may have another cyst and I also wanted to find out about the IVF options. There was indeed a cyst on my ovary, but it was only a simple cyst, so the panic over my endometriosis didn't rear its ugly head. The scan showed good blood flow to my uterus but once again there was a low follicle count. From memory I think there were only two or three follicles on show. The consultant also told me he could see there were some areas of Adenomyosis in my uterus. I was really impressed that he could see that. He was the first doctor ever to mention this based on a scan.

We got a price list and options from the clinic. It was really expensive for two rounds of donor egg IVF; £13,000 in total, and that was using a frozen transfer for the second round in the hope that some embryos were left over for freezing. My gut feeling was we should go with Serum, the Greek clinic that had been so good with me to date, despite never actually going to the clinic in person.

I emailed the lovely Penny for prices at Serum; 5,000 euros for the egg donor and another 1,000 euros for a further frozen transfer which included embryo storage for a year. There was also the legal side of things to consider. In Greece, egg donation was anonymous, but in the UK the child would be able to get information on his/her biological parent at eighteen. Additionally, the Greek clinic had only Greek and Polish donors, whereas the UK had British donors. The waiting time in the UK was 3-6 months at the clinic I was looking into and in Greece there was no waiting time. The Greek clinic guaranteed that all donors young had proven pregnancy/live birth success. Penny was confident she could find a donor with light skin, brown hair and green/blue eyes like myself.

Our gut feeling was to go with the Greek clinic because we had more faith in their abilities to deal with complicated fertility issues and they had a wonderful word of mouth following. My parents stepped in for the last time and offered us the money. They stressed that this would be the last time! So I felt the pressure was on to succeed. Again, we both felt guilty about taking their money.

We made the decision personally to push the issue of anonymity and Greek vs English donor aside, to focus purely on which clinic we thought would give us success.

We planned our first visit to Greece for a week after the Florida holiday, in October. The plan was to go out and suss the clinic out; Mark would give a sperm sample for freezing to fertilise our donor's eggs and I would have an aqua scan done to look at my uterus. We would also have the necessary blood tests done to prove once again we didn't have HIV, HEP B etc, and we would sign consent forms.

The time came for the Florida holiday and it was wonderful; just what I needed. Greece lingered in the backs of our minds during the holiday but we still had a wonderful time, full of memories, the kind that make the lows of the year worth forgetting about for two weeks. While I was in Florida I was so fed up that I was still bleeding some eight months on because of the Depo Provera shot. The shot was supposed to leave me period free and only last three months. Instead it was pure evil! I not only bled everyday but it made me feel dizzy and light-headed at times and I'm sure it made me more anxious. At my wits' end, I decided to Google ways to stop bleeding, since I had already tried medication from my GP and been to a private consultant about all this (he told me to relax and it would sort itself out in time – Arghh!). Mr Google told me to try cinnamon as a natural remedy. So mum and I went on a mission to buy cinnamon in Florida. I got cinnamon sticks and put them in hot water and drank the water; I also took cinnamon tablets, 1000mg in strength. I also ended up buying iron tablets to make me feel better after bleeding all this time. The cinnamon worked a treat, I couldn't believe it. The bleeding stopped, which felt amazing! I had been so miserable before and now I was on Cloud Nine, so happy. Of course it could have been the fact I was on holiday or that I was eight months down the line, but I'm convinced it was the cinnamon. It's definitely worth a try if you're in the same situation that I was in. You can even sprinkle the cinnamon on your food.

We arrived home in October and off we went a week later to Serum in Athens for an initial couple of days. We stayed at the lovely Melia hotel again; it was so nice to see all the familiar faces of the hotel staff and to chat with them. We decided to take taxis this time, as the Athens driving last time was a little crazy and the parking at times difficult. The day after we arrived, in the late evening, we made our way to the clinic. The building was tall and the clinic was laid out over several floors. It was modern and clean inside and all the staff were friendly and nice. We were so surprised at just how organised this clinic was compared to our experience everywhere else. We didn't spend more than five minutes in the waiting room before different members of staff organised our visit. Someone took charge of the forms, and the Gynaecologist, the Phlebotomist, and the reception staff all dealt with us in an efficient and caring manner. Penny wasn't in that day as she had a personal emergency so the Gynaecologist/Surgeon Giannis consulted with us. We confirmed our medical history and that we wished to go ahead with the egg donor route. Mark gave a sperm sample and we were given the option to have a DNA sperm fragmentation test done. This would determine if the genetic material within the sperm was abnormal, which in turn could lead to male subfertility and IVF failure. We thought it would be really important to get this done so we went ahead with the test, along with the normal sperm analysis, followed by freezing of the sperm. We waited a day for the result of this test. I highly recommend this test if you haven't considered it. We asked the consultant what could be done if the test was bad news and they said a course of antibiotics might improve sperm quality.

I went on to have an aqua scan, which involves a saline solution through into the uterus to highlight any problems. You uterus is supposed to expand with the saline solution but it was immediately apparent my uterus was not expanding, which Giannis explained wasn't as he would expect. I asked why would it not expand and he said it was an indication of scarring. I immediately felt angry and let down because the hysteroscopy I had done privately during my laparoscopy surgery three months prior showed no issues with my uterus. How could the consultant in the UK tell me I had a good uterus when I in fact didn't?

Giannis sat us down in the office and suggested we do a hysteroscopy with implantation cuts at the private maternity hospital the next morning, with him as my surgeon. He explained that the effects of the hysteroscopy, including implantation cuts, would provide around eight months of improved condition of the uterus and sometimes the procedure alone is enough to help spontaneous pregnancy, where implantation failure was a factor due to the condition of the uterus. First of all we were both in shock with the results of the scan. We had to think fast; it was 4 pm and he was suggesting surgery at 7 am the next day. I felt scared; I didn't expect to have surgery on this trip. This would never happen in the UK, I thought, an offer of surgery the next day just like that; now that is efficient. I think Serum have an excellent working relationship with the Mitera hospital. I had to call my parents and ask if they could fund the 1,650 euros for the surgery. Of course they agreed; it needed to be done or the IVF might turn out to be a waste of time. The receptionist booked the theatre slot for the surgery next morning and the hospital pre-op tests. We needed to leave straightaway in the taxi so I could have the pre-op tests done. Once at the Mitera hospital I was taken straight in to be seen; no waiting around. I had bloods taken, an ECG test, I was weighed and measured, all the standard tests. Everyone was friendly and spoke English. The hospital was clean and had a cafeteria open 24 hours, a bank, cash machine, post box and a gift shop.

After the hospital we took a taxi at the taxi rank outside the front door back to our hotel. It felt like a whirlwind of a day but highly productive. I suggest that if you go for the aqua scan at Serum, be prepared; you may be having a hysteroscopy the next day at the local hospital.

The following morning we woke up at 6 am; I wasn't allowed to eat and we were in a rush to leave at 6.30 am to be at the hospital for 7 am, where we would meet Giannis. The hotel was wonderful, packing our breakfasts in boxes to take with us since we had already paid for breakfast as part of our room rate. It was great and I planned to eat mine straight after the surgery. It had sandwiches, fruit, pastries, water and juice. I was a little nervous but felt reassured that I'd seen the hospital, met my surgeon and was in good hands.

When we arrived at the hospital I waited five minutes and then went straight in to get my operating gown on and be

The Infertility Crossroads

checked by the nurse. I was then wheeled through to the corridor, where I waited with my surgeon to go into the operating room, which was currently being used. The anaesthetist introduced herself and I got a cannula put in my arm. I remember everyone was friendly and some of the surgeons had nice patterns on their head scarfs. As I waited in the corridor I saw a few babies come out of the delivery theatre suites; they had just been born. I heard that new-born, first ever baby cry. The babies each had three members of staff and a high-tech baby incubator. I presume they were off to the NICU. It was nice to see they were being so well taken care of.

Soon it was my turn to go in. I was transferred onto the theatre bed and had my legs in stirrups like at a gynaecologist's office. It seemed a bit strange that I had my hands and legs strapped down, but it was practical, so that I wouldn't fall once I was asleep. I remember seeing the screen which would be used to display the image from the camera they put into my uterus; the procedure would be filmed to show me on DVD after the operation. They told me I was being put to sleep by the medicine going into my cannula and I did my usual, kept my eyes open as long as possible and placed myself on a beach.

When I woke up I remember being in a recovery room with staff attending to me. They asked me how I felt and I told them my stomach hurt. They explained it was just the anaesthetic and they told me not to worry, they would give me some medicine in my cannula to help. It worked fast and the pain went away. I think I was in recovery for half an hour. I remember looking at the clock the whole time and I couldn't focus my eyes enough to read the time until they were just about to move me to my room and the anaesthetic had started to wear off.

The Infertility Crossroads

I was taken in the lift up to a ward and given a bed. I shared the room with one other patient and it had its own bathroom. I had a button to call the nurse if I needed anything and the caterer came with food for me. I rested for a short while and was reunited with Mark, who'd been waiting in the cafeteria and waiting room. I had used the bedside phone to ask someone to call my husband up. I felt fine shortly afterwards and I got out of bed and discharged myself. We went straight back to Serum and by this time it was lunchtime.

Giannis was back at the clinic and when we sat down to chat, in walked Penny. It was so lovely to finally meet her and she was just how I imagined; warm, friendly and full of knowledge. The results came back normal for the sperm DNA fragmentation, which was a relief, one less problem to face. Then we sat down and watched the DVD of my operation. Wow, there was scar tissue everywhere, and infection. Giannis explained there was no way an embryo could implant; it would not be able to find the blood supply to implant, with all the scar tissue and also chronic Chlamydia infection. I watched as he used an instrument to cut implantation cuts into the top of the uterus, then he proceeded to do a D&C to remove all the scar tissue. How did my surgeon in June miss all of this? I had no idea! At least we had Giannis sorting me out now. It was well worth the money and I can highly recommend the procedure to others. The way Giannis explained things to us, the egg had to be good, the sperm had to be good and the uterus had to be good to make a baby. These were the three elements. It made sense to us. I felt like I had wasted my time on the three rounds of IVF before now, because of the bad condition my uterus was in.

After our chat I left the clinic with a bag full of medicine. The plan was to delay the IVF for a month because I would be taking antibiotics post-surgery, a month's worth of antibiotic for the infection and then the pre-treatment plan followed by the start of my IVF, one and a half months later. Even though I had taken the antibiotics ten months previously for hidden Chlamydia, because it was a chronic infection it had come back and would continue to come back unless suppressed by antibiotics.

Later that same day we flew back home and began the medication programme. Mark commended me for being so brave at the airport and I really appreciated that he said that to me.

Upon arriving home I organised my medication on the kitchen worktop. I had to take the brown Cyclacur and Prixina tablets for ten days following the hysteroscopy and the supplement Serrapeptase, which also has anti-inflammatory effects, to help dissolve scar tissue. This supplement was to be taken twice a day and the tablets were quite large. I remember feeling slightly uncomfortable taking these on an empty stomach. I then went on to a round of medication to get rid of my chronic infection. This included taking the antibiotic Azithromycin, which was a horrible drug. It gave me terrible stomach ache and diarrhoea for at least the whole morning. I was also taking Doxycycline; not to mention the other tablets I took, such as prenatal vitamins and my life saver probiotic called Biokult. This works wonders! I recommend it to everyone. I take one a day normally to keep my stomach happy and for my general health but if I'm ever on antibiotics or travelling on a plane I take four a day. If I'm on antibiotics and I take four Biokult a day they stop me from getting thrush, which always used to coincide with antibiotics because antibiotics kill all the good bacteria as well as the bad, but these tablets replenished the good bacteria that are lost.

The Infertility Crossroads

The antibiotic protocol felt relentless but necessary; more to the point, I had to really organise my medication schedule. I was taking two types of antibiotics, prenatal vitamins, probiotics, Serrapeptase and some medications were on different days, different times, multiple times per day. Mark felt really sorry for me. I did feel positive I was doing all the right things, getting through the programme of meds. I'd always feel elated and excited moving onto the next programme. I then started the pre-treatment plan. I'd be taking Prednizolone (steroid) twice a day and Celebrex (anti-inflammatory) to combat my endometriosis, plus a high dose of folic acid (5mg). This was all on top of the prenatal multivitamin, Biokult and Serrapeptase. Then the time came for me to down regulate my cycle so my husband had to inject me in the bum with Arvekap. This was to suppress me from ovulating as I was using a donor egg, and also to suppress my endometriosis. The effects from this injection would last four weeks. It made me anxious over what happened last time I had a down regulation injection, which was only supposed to last three months but messed my cycle up for eight months. I did hum and ha a bit as to whether I should have this injection and Penny emailed me back with reassurance that I would be fine. I am happy to confirm I was fine, no side effects and it didn't mess up my cycle. I kept in touch with Penny on email and finally the exciting news came, the information on our lovely donor. The kind of information we received was about her age, hair and eye colour, height and build, skin colour, personal character/nature, education level, hobbies and interests. She was an excellent match for us; I have to say the clinic did a wonderful job finding her. Mark and I prepared a letter saying how grateful we were to her for doing this for us and we also bought a piece of jewellery for her. We would give it to the clinic to pass on to her as we were not allowed to meet. I actually felt more at ease and happy once I had a bit of insight into our donor, and I couldn't help but think of what she might be going through, having been through it all myself.

I was now ready to start the donor egg protocol to get me ready for transfer of our embryos. At this stage, of course, we didn't know how many eggs would be collected or embryos made, but the clinic would guarantee a top quality blastocyst embryo, which was reassuring, and, as I said before, the donors were all proven to have had a pregnancy. I started taking Cyclacur (to thicken the lining of my uterus), folic acid, Prednisolone (steroid), Salospir (blood thinner like Aspirin to provide good blood supply to the uterus), Doxycycline (antibiotic) and Valtrex (to suppress the HHV6 virus sometimes found in patients with infertility). The clinic continued to up the dose of Cyclacur in increments and then I had a scan locally to assess the thickness of the lining of my uterus. I think it needed to be above 7mm. The day of the scan I was a bit nervous but I had never had a problem in the past with the thickness of the lining of my uterus. I paid £60 for my scan and the lady who did it was ever so nice. My lining was 9mm, which I was really happy with; I emailed the clinic with the results and they were also happy. I recommend shopping around for scan clinics because prices can be double this in some of them. When I was at the ultrasound clinic the lady who did my scan told me that a lot of women coming into her clinic who suffered infertility and got pregnant used a supplement called Inofolic. I told her I would look into this. I asked my consultant about this product and she told me it was predominantly for women with PCOS but it also regulates your monthly cycle, aids weight loss in women with PCOS and improves egg quality, so I thought it was worth mentioning. I wasn't in a position to try it at that moment. It is also worth mentioning that I didn't have enough Valtrex tablets and I couldn't get the prescription in time in the post from Greece, as it took about a week. There are companies in the UK who take the email form of the prescription but they charge a lot for delivery, like £35-50 on top of the cost of the drugs. My advice is to try and get some drugs through the NHS. I went to my local GUM clinic and got the Valtrex for free, which saved me £130. Valtrex is needed to suppress the HHV6 virus, which is from the herpes family; that's why the GUM clinic supplied it. I also managed to get the GUM clinic to do our infection screening once, and it only cost me £50 for the NHS to provide the letter, compared to £200 for both of us getting bloods elsewhere.

After the scan we were given the date for our donor's egg collection and the date for transfer, so we could finally book our flights and hotel. We were getting excited now. It was nearly Christmas and we were off to Greece to try for a baby; it felt magical. I'd already figured out that my test date would be Christmas day. We thought this would be the best Christmas present ever! Every year Christmas would come by and still no children in the house, or even a pregnancy. It was difficult because Christmas was a time for family and children enjoy Christmas the most. Seeing those happy little faces on children at Christmas would have been wonderful. The flip side of the test date being Christmas day was if it failed I would be devastated and there is nothing worse than feeling sad and empty on Christmas day. I felt under pressure; if I needed support from clinics for tests they would largely be shut down over the Christmas period. Looking back, I honestly don't recommend carrying out IVF during the latter part of December or the first week in January. It's just not good timing and is actually quite stressful. Most people are also full of emotions at the end of the old year and the beginning of a new year; often, feeling like we are going into the unknown of the next year and saying goodbye to the good and bad feelings of the last year can be hard.

The Infertility Crossroads

I kept in touch with Penny to see how our donor was doing and the good news started to roll in. We got ten eggs and seven had fertilised. I was confident at this point that some would make it to blastocyst stage. This trip to Greece we had to stay in a hotel at Heathrow airport the night before as the flight was early. We didn't get a good night's sleep, unfortunately, due to the bed in the hotel and we were quite tired that day, with all the travel on top of a bad sleep. We were at the clinic the next day for the embryo transfer, which was at lunchtime. However, we had to go early because there were people protesting on the streets outside our hotel that morning; it was stressing me out hearing all the chanting, plus they were blocking the streets. We had to walk a couple of blocks to get a taxi but once we got to the neighbourhood of the clinic there were all the usual amenities, like Starbucks (where we chilled), supermarket, bank, restaurants, pharmacies etc. After chilling in Starbucks we went for our embryo transfer. Again the staff were very attentive and well organised. We got the exciting news that we had four day five embryos; two were AA grade, one AB and one they felt we should let grow an extra day to catch up. We decided to transfer the two best embryos, the AA grade.

I felt much more relaxed than during all my previous embryo transfers in other clinics. The room was very warm, which I liked and made me feel more comfortable; I was naked from the waist down except for a sheet to cover me. Penny was doing the transfer, which I was happy about. She explained that the warm room was good; embryos don't like to be cold or outside the range of body temperature for long, which made sense. Penny was a pro at the embryo transfer; she explained everything clearly, and I could watch on the ultrasound screen and actually see two flickers of white against the black background as she put the two embryos in. She carefully placed them where she could see the implantation cuts from my operation. We were given an ultrasound picture showing our two embryos in place, which was a nice touch. Penny managed to carry out the procedure without pain and I was amazed! The experience was nothing like my three previous embryo transfers.

Next I had a blood test for my progesterone level, which came back fine, and I was left to rest for half an hour while I had Intralipids infused. Intralipids stimulate the immune system to remove 'danger signals' that can lead to pregnancy loss. A member of staff went through the work with my customised programme of meds during the two-week wait and also further instructions to get me up to three months of pregnancy if we were successful. I was provided with more medication to cover this period.

We both felt happy with how the treatment had gone and we went for lunch afterwards at TGI Fridays; it was good food and the same friendly staff we saw on our previous trips to Greece. I rested later that day, back in our hotel room, and we enjoyed room service. The Greek food was delicious! I downloaded the Zita West Positive Visualisation listening exercises on iTunes and they really helped. I would often fall asleep listening to them, which showed how relaxed I was. I also tried to stay warm with layered clothing and blankets. The next day we flew home and it really felt like the two-week wait had begun. We also got the good news that our other embryo had turned out to be another AA grade. So we had this embryo and the other AB one frozen together for a possible future transfer.

The two-week wait didn't get any easier fourth time around. In fact it only felt harder. Christmas was a bit of a distraction, what with wrapping presents, Christmas food shopping and putting up the Christmas tree. I joined the Serum Athens IVF support group on Facebook. It was a world of comfort and a way to connect with other people at the clinic or who were contemplating going to SERUM for treatment. We could all empathise with each other and shared our knowledge of the treatments available. I highly recommend infertility support groups on Facebook; they connect you with people who really do understand you and your own personal struggles.

The second week of the two-week wait was especially hard, and then came the few days before Christmas. I tested early on a home pregnancy test and it was negative. I was feeling really low and sat and cried! In my heart I knew it hadn't worked; the chances of the test changing between then and Christmas day were slim. I tried to warn Mark and my mum it wasn't looking good and my mum in particular was really upset, but Mark was still hopeful.

When Christmas day came the test was still negative. It was all over! I cried and cried and my husband comforted me again. All our hopes and dreams had been shattered again. The embryos were really good quality. What happened? It was Christmas day and my parents were coming round for Christmas lunch, so I rang them to tell them the bad news. I felt really bad telling them. I felt I'd let everyone down again. I decided I had no choice but to put on a brave face and try and enjoy what was left of Christmas day. To my amazement we had a great Christmas lunch and afternoon playing games and watching TV. I definitely think it put everyone else at ease because they would have been tip-toeing around me if not and I didn't want that. I emailed the clinics I had booked my blood tests and Intralipids at and cancelled the appointments. At least we had one more attempt. Maybe we were just unlucky.

I emailed the clinic with the bad news and they were very sad to hear it hadn't worked. Collectively we decided to go straight into another round of IVF; I had responded well to the medication and it was still in my body, suppressing my immune system etc. I had to wait a few days for my period to turn up, and when it did it was really light compared to other failed IVF cycles before the laparoscopy surgery. I think the surgery really helped. I continued with the same protocol as last time. We researched to see if there was anything we could do to improve the cycle this time. I wanted to make sure my immune system wasn't the factor causing my failure to implant, despite being on steroids already. I spoke to Penny and she told me I could have the Chicago immune test done when I next flew out for embryo transfer. It was a straightforward blood test costing 390 euros. They would be testing for NK cells, NK cytotoxicity assay and Th1/Th2 intracellular cytokine ratios. I felt positive that I had found another test which might give us the key to success.

The other difference with this cycle was that I tried an anti-inflammatory diet to help with my uterus condition and endometriosis. I would eat walnuts, pineapple, chai seeds, flax seeds, bok choy, brazil nuts, leafy greens, chicken, pork, eggs, fish, ginger and turmeric tea, healthy fats like olive oil, raspberry leaf tea (great for the uterus before IVF) and low carbs (sticking to the non-processed carbs like potatoes and wholegrain rice). I tried to buy organic where possible. I cut out red meat like mince and I cut out processed and sugary foods. I felt really good while on my anti-inflammatory diet. It did feel like a lot of cooking and meal planning, but it was worth it. My mum helped me a lot with making sure I had ingredients for new recipes and helping me source organic where possible. I think she enjoyed helping me because she felt that it was one way she could get involved and help me. If you're going through this and trying a special food diet, perhaps getting your mum involved is a good idea. I know my mum loved it and it's a way for them to feel like they can help you. Plus mums are normally more experienced cooks with new ideas and recipes. Try not to get stressed out over it, though. I did at times because I put this enormous pressure on myself to eat the right things, but at the end of the day if the IVF wants to work it will work for multiple reasons and not diet alone. I knew someone who was going through IVF at the time and got pregnant while eating lots of junk food, but I followed my diet to feel better and because I knew I was prone to inflammatory responses in my body, like endometriosis.

It was the end of December when I started the medication and a week later the time came to get my lining thickness scan at the clinic in the UK. I felt embarrassed and sad walking in to get my scan. The lady remembered me and was really nice; she said straightaway she could tell I was sad. She really did try to cheer me up, which was sweet, and she wanted me to keep in touch and let her know how things went. I thought, great! If I have a baby I'll definitely be back to have my scans here and share the miraculous news; but if not how am I supposed to ring her and tell her it didn't work? I would feel so much shame and sadness. Anyway, the good news was my scan was a good thickness, over 9mm, so I was happy.

We flew out to Greece a week later; by this point the process of getting to the airport, parking the car, making our way through the terminal, flying, taxi, and hotel was second nature. Greece really does feel like a second home for us and the people are so friendly! We enjoyed the warmer climate and blue skies; considering it was January, at least there was no snow and the sun was out, but it was definitely cooler than during our December visit. This trip my negative thoughts and low self-esteem regarding the whole IVF process left me on the floor. I just could not seem to pick myself up. I felt kind of numb to it all. Every now and again I'd check in with my own thoughts and feel guilty over how I was feeling. Why was I not happy? I had another chance of becoming a mother; but it just felt so hard because I couldn't believe it would be different this time.

While we were out in Greece I focused on eating the right things, the foods I had researched online. I manage to source pomegranate juice, pineapple (remembering to eat the core too), and Brazil nuts. All of these foods are supposed to be good for implantation and a healthy uterus.

The day of embryo transfer went well and I had my blood test done for the Chicago Test, along with my progesterone level. I was put on Intralipids again after the embryo transfer. My progesterone level came back fine and I waited a few days for the results of the Chicago test. We ate lunch at our usual TGI Fridays, a short distance from the clinic. I was still feeling a bit numb emotionally from the whole process.

We watched movies that night at the hotel and I wore the extra thick socks I had bought for this time around. I got the socks from an outdoor pursuits shop and they had a 2.3 tog rating, like a duvet. The Chinese believe that keeping your feet warm ensures a warm womb, so it was worth a try, plus I enjoyed having warm feet for once. The socks stayed with me for the whole two-week wait.

That evening in the hotel we were sitting in our room on the sixth floor when an earthquake hit. It was 4.6 on the Richter scale and the room shook. We could hear the rubble falling down the cavity in the walls. It quickly ended and we were fine. Luckily it didn't happen again, but it was such a surreal experience!

When we got back to the UK I went into work, looking after the one–year-old in my care, but I didn't feel anything other than stress. I went to the doctor the next day and got signed off work for stress for two weeks. I had just started to come around to the idea of being in this 'pregnant until proven otherwise' state. I was happy and feeling over-protective. The test results came back from the Chicago test. I had slightly raised NK cell levels, which meant if I was to get pregnant after implantation I would need to up the dose of steroids to two tablets a day. I was happy to have found out this useful information.

Then all of a sudden my stress level went from 50mph to 100mph as my employer told me I was being made redundant. I literally couldn't cope. I was a mess. In the middle of my two-week wait the last thing I needed to be thinking about was my job security. There was the money for the baby or the money for another IVF attempt (if this failed), and on top of that the standard bills that roll in every month. My husband felt the strain massively too, and to be completely honest the TWW (two-week wait) felt like a train wreck. I had all these pregnancy symptoms and now I was so emotional, trying to resolve my job situation when I was supposed to be on stress leave. I had massive bruises on my legs from the Clexane injections, too, which I sought advice from my doctor's surgery about. We found that putting the needle in at a slight angle helped reduce the bruising, but it was ultimately the nature of the blood thinner itself.

The day came for my HCG blood test to find out if I was pregnant. I decided this time I was going to avoid the pee stick test and get the blood test; the clinic wanted a definitive blood test result, including progesterone level this time.

I left feeling really happy that morning. I kissed Mark and off I went to the local fertility clinic. The test results would come back that afternoon. The day felt very long and time dragged a bit.

Late that afternoon I received a phone call with the results. It was negative again. I started to cry as I put the phone down. I actually couldn't believe it; my whole world shattered. I was convinced that it had worked this time, but it hadn't. I tried to compose myself as I rang my husband at work to tell him the bad news. His immediate reaction was, 'You're joking!' I told him I was sorry and he said I had nothing to be sorry about. I felt so bad for him being at work and receiving this horrible news, but he insisted I called him. He wasn't going to be home from work till near midnight and so I ended up having my parents come over to console me. I asked for some junk food to eat, so we sat and ate burgers and ice cream. The healthy eating went straight out the window and in came the comfort food! They were upset too, and I felt bad for them. I felt like I was in so much pain my heart could burst. I really was inconsolable. That night I went to bed in tears and in the morning I woke early, at 6 am, only to find that Mark wasn't in the bed; he hadn't come home that night at all. I was so worried! For the first time in my whole relationship my husband didn't come home for three nights. I have never been so ill in my entire life! My stomach churned and made me so ill and I couldn't stop crying. I barely ate or drank anything for days. I knew he was devastated and I couldn't comfort him. I missed his comfort terribly. I went from being sad over my loss to being even sadder over Mark not coming home. The sense of loss was overwhelming! I was also worrying because I hadn't had my period and what if my embryo had implanted late? My friend came over and tried to cheer me up; she brought some food, which was so lovely of her. I'm sure my stomach had shrunk from not eating so I couldn't eat much.

I didn't leave the house for three days waiting for Mark to come home. I ended up speaking to the lovely Penny at the clinic over the phone. She told me she was completely baffled at the failure of the procedure. This was the first time the donor had not had success with her eggs. Penny kept referring to me as a baby, as I was still young at twenty-eight, and she desperately didn't want to recommend we go down the double donor or adoption route. She suggested perhaps there was something wrong with my husband's sperm that there wasn't a test invented for yet. She referred to it as a hidden sperm problem. She kept going over the fact that we had four good embryos and how strange it was that at least one didn't implant. Why was I failing to get past that point? Perhaps the damage caused by Mark's undescended testicles was irreparable. Penny suggested we could try one last time with my own eggs and a sperm donor, or try with a different egg donor. The final option would be a double donor or embryo adoption, leaving us with no genetic tie to our child.

When Mark finally came back I felt so relieved. I just wanted to hold him. We talked over everything that had happened and we found comfort in each other again. I felt both traumatised and relieved at the same time. Mark felt really sad about the news from Penny; it is a massive blow for any man to hear the news that his sperm might not be good enough to continue the family name and have a family with his wife.

My period arrived and made everything feel final; it was over.

The Greek trips cost, in total, around £9,000, by the time you add all the additional tests, medication, procedures, flights, hotel, taxis and food. It was a loss in itself and more money down the drain, with still no baby or even a hint of pregnancy.

17. Family perspectives

I wanted to include a chapter about the thoughts and feelings of my husband, and mum. It was something I constantly thought and worried about. I didn't really start to understand the full impact it had on their lives until the middle of our infertility journey, especially from my mum's point of view. While it affects every family differently, I'm sure you'll find it insightful to see how it affected our family dynamic. My family couldn't live their lives without feeling hurt and pain for us.

Written by my Mum...

This is a chapter that no parents should ever have to write, but I as Heather's mum, and my husband, write this to hopefully help and support the many others that are going through, or are planning on going through, treatment for infertility.

We have supported our daughter and her husband along the way, so we wanted to contribute to this book, so courageously written by Heather.

My husband and I have always provided our time and financial support, as and when required, throughout the lives of our two children, and of course this infertility issue is an expensive exercise and we were able to buy into this, but money can't buy a guaranteed solution. We gave an ear to all the terminology about IVF, which, to be quite honest, was mind-blowing, and I have to confess there was an awful amount that I could never get my head around.

The Infertility Crossroads

We supported them through the hurdles of possible adoption, but this isn't the easiest of routes either, and can be very impersonal in oh so many ways. We had a social worker come to visit us and we wrote a reference to support their application. We also went to an evening held by the adoption team aimed at extended family members.

There are so many different types of infertility and to get to the root cause of the issue can take many attempts, as you learn along the way; and finding the right clinic and practitioners can be a matter of luck. So be prepared for a long journey unless you are one of the lucky ones. But also, if you are the ones providing funding, be realistic and look at all the medical advice. Be gentle and offer your company when required and keep your cherished ones as close as they will allow, or need.

Be prepared for heartache. I suffered heartaches with all the attempts that failed. I write this chapter on a wet and windy February day, realising that a baby of their own will possibly never happen and that the final attempt is over, or at least it seems that way now.

However, I know our daughter to be a strong person and along with her husband, they will get on with their lives, building a new framework from their preferred choice of their own family, but just as I wait for spring and all its beauties to arrive I trust they will have a beautiful life together.

Written by my Husband…

Our infertility journey has been an emotional rollercoaster. I thought having a baby was going to be easy, a walk in the park. Instead it's hit or miss whether or not it works, as unfortunately medical science doesn't yet have all the answers.

The Infertility Crossroads

For me personally, having a family means bringing someone into the world who is an extension of me and my wife. It would be special if we had a boy and he could continue on with my name. Watching them grow up and concentrating on them instead of other things in my life would be wonderful. Watching them being happy, would make me happy.

The first time we attempted IVF I was hopeful and positive, like you just know you're going to win the lottery! The second time you think you've made the right changes to different doctors and clinics and perhaps that will make it work this time, but then it doesn't. Suddenly the process becomes more monotonous.

Watching my wife go through IVF and surgery made me feel sad, and angry at the suffering she went through. All I had to do was produce a sperm sample in a pot. I felt powerless and helpless, with no answers.

Why should I feel something when I didn't have the treatment? How do I have the right to feel anything when I didn't feel the pain, I only felt the result? In a selfish way I'm glad I didn't have to go through all that because I don't think I could be that strong. I'd ask myself at the end of every failed round: was it all worth it when it fails?

Seeing your wife bruised from needles and gaining weight from water retention etc, was hard. I would have to bear the brunt of it all emotionally and have to keep a brave face on for my wife; but that's just what I had to do, hold it together for both of us.

If you're going through treatment right now, to all the men I would say; be there and be supportive. Tell your wife she looks good. If she has a go at you because of her hormones, don't make a deal of it, just let it go. Your wife may be thinking she's disappointed you when it fails and blame herself, especially when the money's gone down the drain as well as the loss of embryo(s). Forget about the money side of it, no one is to blame, no one is letting each other down, you committed when you married that person, and children are a bonus. Finally buy a pet, like a cat, as they are wonderfully therapeutic.

To all the women out there; your husband may act like he doesn't give a toss but there are times when it fails and there is nothing you can say to make it better, you're lost for words. IVF made me angry, it is a massive upheaval in your life, it is a massive commitment in your daily routine, injecting your wife, appointments etc. It's an emotional burden; if you're a man and you really want to have children through fertility treatment, it involves attending to your wife and being sympathetic all the time, and that's challenging long-term because in a sense you become an emotional carer for her wellbeing.

My advice for you, if you're seeking more fertility treatment, is to make sure your IVF cycle is tailor-made for you. You may have one issue, you may have several; we are all different, so it shouldn't be a 'one size fits all' approach. If you've done three, four, five rounds of IVF and you as a man don't want to do it again because you see it affecting your relationship, you should take a break. Your wife needs that break to set the emotionally highly charged feelings back to neutral. Give it a break and you'll come back together as a couple. Then you can decide what you want to do next. If anything hold your wife closer.

In the future I want us to be happy with the decisions we've made, knowing that we've done everything we can do. Knowing that IVF is an ever-changing science and maybe one day we will have what we want or we can be open-minded to other paths. You've got to be happy in life.

18. Deciding how and when to move on

The pain that followed our fifth attempt at IVF was excruciating. Yes, along our journey and in my life I've felt the pain of grief, but I've never known pain quite the same as the pain that followed. At the start of our journey I collapsed to the floor from the shock of realising our infertility. I've expressed tears of disappointment, tears of anger, but this was different. It was the kind of pain that tears the soul and leaves it wide open to being vulnerable at just a moment's notice.

I felt physically and emotionally ill for a solid week following our fifth failure. Then without thinking (which was strange for me because all my decisions were based on weighing up facts and carefully deciding on things) I chose my life and my husband. I really do mean it, I didn't think to make that decision, it just came to me like a ray of sunshine, feeding my soul, and I felt instant happiness and warmth. It was an epiphany. I love my husband, I loved him the moment I saw him and I couldn't lose him. He is more important to me than any child because he is here right now and he has always been. He needs to feel loved, he needs to know I am and can be the woman he fell in love with, because he deserves that. Now I know that some of you reading this book may choose to leave your husband if he doesn't stand by you in your quest for a child and that's okay, if that's what you really want. It has to be okay to say: this is my life and this is what makes me happy! Yes, sometimes compromise is needed. We've had plenty of compromise in our marriage so far and that's worked out well for us. Life is short; I've learned that along the way. I've watched loved ones die while I've been on a quest to bring life into this world. Don't waste a minute

The Infertility Crossroads

looking back in regret at the decisions you've made. Live for today, live for this moment; as cheesy as that may sound, it's true when you think of what it really means. There is always someone less fortunate than us out there in the world and our health can be taken away at any moment.

The week following the tearing apart of my soul I went out on date nights with Mark. I leapt around the house like Tigger. I called my personal trainer and went back to seeing her once a week. Additionally, I started going to the gym by myself and also with Mark. I do around three sessions of exercise a week to keep me feeling more energetic, and motivated, to get my body back from all the ill-effects of IVF, and to feel happy afterwards. I made amends with the family I worked for. I forgave them for their bad timing and chose to cherish the friendship with them that had formed over the last year. Mark and I hid ourselves away from family and focused on just us, communicating all our thoughts and feelings. Reconnecting! It is so important to reconnect and I don't mean just, 'how was your day?' I mean telling your partner, 'Remember we used to go to the cinema and eat pic & mix and ice cream? We should do that again. I really enjoyed doing that with you!' These are the small details of happy times that spark a smile on one another's faces. Get your love life back, because IVF ruins all that. The very thing that makes making a baby fun is the first thing to be spoiled. It ruins your self-confidence, your energy levels, and then there are the two-week waits where no sex is allowed etc. Sometimes reconnecting means: just lying next to each other with your arms round each other and crying. Words don't have to be spoken; sometimes words aren't needed. It's our hearts which speak to one another through our energy of love. The moment of sadness will pass and you'll start a conversation on some random topic, but at least you had that moment to grieve together.

We experienced the five stages of grief and loss during our journey many times over.

These are the five stages of grief and loss:

1. Denial and Isolation ('This isn't happening, this can't be happening');
2. Anger (Anger may be aimed at inanimate objects, complete strangers, friends, family or a medical professional);
3. Bargaining (If only statements, 'If only we had sought medical attention sooner');
4. Depression (The private farewell to our embryo/eggs/sperm that didn't make it or farewell and sadness to our infertility);
5. Acceptance (Reaching this stage of grieving is a gift not afforded to everyone, it's a feeling of calm).

We may not all go through these stages of grief in the same order; we also may go backwards in our journey through grief or skip a stage because time is limited, and we don't have time to feel the final stages of grief. Throughout each stage, a common thread of hope emerges: As long as there is life, there is hope. As long as there is hope, there is life.

Allow yourself to feel the grief when it comes; and it comes in waves. When the waves are high, notice the emotions you are feeling, take time for yourself. Look after yourself. I always remember a friend saying, 'mind yourself'; I now know this is what she meant. Then when the moment passes and the wave is flat, go for a walk to shake it off and then move on with your day. You'll feel elated that you survived this wave and you know you will survive the next wave, even if it is emotionally draining and difficult. You never know when the next one may hit you, but

The Infertility Crossroads

as time passes, the waves will be fewer and farther between.

Time will heal ... I have always believed this. The passing of time allows us to process things that have happened, our thoughts and feelings; and when we allow ourselves to do this we can continue to move on and live life.

I don't know your personal story and so I'm speaking very broadly here. You may be at the beginning of your journey. Your first treatment has failed and you're in disbelief it didn't work; or you may be further down the line in number of attempts at treatment than I went. I share one thing with you all, though: the ability to sympathise with you wherever you are in your journey.

Deciding how and when to move on is a difficult bridge to cross. The reason I shared our journey was to show that our own individual journey was always evolving, always changing. Our journey is entirely unique to us as individuals and as a couple.

There were times when we were not on the same page together and one of us would have to wait for the other to catch up. You may not be on the same page as your partner right now, which is really tough on you both. Be patient and be kind. Patience is the hardest thing to achieve, particularly as a woman, as you watch your egg reserve deplete each month. You feel like you're watching the clock. Be kind to one another, as Ellen Degeneres always says. You are both dealing with a lot, so please be kind. I watch the Ellen Degeneres show every weekday and it really cheers me up and distracts me from my own life. I highly recommend watching the show because Ellen truly has a way of cheering others up and putting a smile on so many people's faces around the world.

The Infertility Crossroads

To decide how you will move forward in your own personal journey to have a family will require you to process your grief and loss first, to some degree. You can't decide overnight how you will move on; it will be a process of many conversations, some long and some short. Try not to put a time frame on how long these conversations have to go on for. It may be a week, a month, or years. You may be thinking about how you carry on with your lives, just the two of you, and live life to the max; or you may be considering trying more tests, treatment, IVF, or even choosing to adopt or foster.

A lot of your reasoning will come down to why you wanted children in the first place. Think about the reasons we choose to have children: you love babies and children, because it's natural; someone to carry on the family name, someone to look after us when we are older; you wanted to experience pregnancy and childbirth, to let your children (who don't exist yet) experience the joy of existence; to give your parents grandchildren; to have a sibling for your child/children; to have a cousin for your brother or sister's children; to embody love for another human being; to relive your own childhood and personally grow and mature from these experiences.

If you choose to move on entirely from having children then I would say this. In my opinion, it is worth paying for every test you feel you need, having every treatment you've gone through or need to go through, and it is definitely worth speaking with a counsellor to seek some sort of peace with the idea that you did everything you could. You gave it your all and you can feel proud of yourself. Even if counselling costs thousands of pounds, if it's worth it to you and enables you to live your life, then do it. At that point it's about getting your life back and feeling in control again; because, let's face it, infertility does not make you feel in control.

The Infertility Crossroads

Spend your money on making memories or things that make you happy. Get stuck into a project like decorating your house. Change your career to a more fulfilling one, even if that means you go back to some sort of education. Make new friends, perhaps with others who don't have children. Travel the world and smile every time you realise how tricky this would have been with a child by your side. Be kind to others by volunteering or giving to others; it will make you feel good. We once surprised my parents when they came back from Florida by replacing and installing a new dishwasher that they needed; and we also pressure washed their patio, which went from black to a lovely sandy colour. It meant the world to them and their faces were priceless.

Spend time with your nieces or nephews. Get back the time you wanted to spend with them when, unfortunately, you were dealing with your own infertility. I remember once walking my nephew, aged three, to the local shop and buying him an ice cream, and greatly enjoying such a simple outing with him. The look on his face made it all worthwhile.

Make yourself look and feel nice again. Perhaps indulge in a new hairstyle, get your make-up done at the local make-up counter, have a massage. Get a new wardrobe of clothes or just sort through your old wardrobe.

Take up some new hobbies and challenge yourself. My husband wants to learn to fly a plane. This is one of his life-long ambitions.

At some point I recommend you hold a small ceremony in a park or garden. Plant something in memory of the child you may never have. It helps to let go and aids with the grieving process. You will always feel your loss to some degree. Like on Mother's Day, for example, or something that reminds you of your loss; it is perfectly normal to feel

The Infertility Crossroads

like that and we are all only human. It's just like when we miss the loved ones we may have lost. You will, however, reach the point of peace eventually, and things will get better and you will feel happier.

If you choose to continue with fertility treatment, keeping a diary with your thoughts and feelings is a good way of letting off steam and processing your emotions.

Seek out a second or third opinion, even if that means a different clinic. Do your research and make sure you have the right investigatory tests done before spending huge sums of money on IVF. That is one thing we would have done differently if we had the chance.

Do your research and challenge any clinic you go with to perform all the necessary diagnostic tests. Make sure they have a good quality scanner. If you have one shot left on the NHS to try IVF, make it count by doing all the necessary diagnostic testing first. It will probably be as expensive as one round of IVF but it will save money and heartache down the line if you have most of the answers up front; and it will give you a clearer indication of what might work for you as a couple.

Be prepared for the possibility that you may have to let go of a genetic tie to your child on one or both sides if you truly want to walk away with a baby at the end of the process. You may even need a surrogate. Try and imagine how many more times you might need or want to try, and the financial impact that might have on you as a couple. It is better to be realistic in advance, rather than screaming at each other over money troubles down the line. Perhaps you might be better off going for an IVF refund programme or a pregnancy guarantee programme. These are programmes where you either walk away with a baby for x amount of money or you get your money back. These schemes usually include three or four rounds of treatment within an 18-month period. Be prepared for the toll this will take on your body and the time off work needed for a programme like this.

Don't forget to give time to one another, getting on with the usual activities you enjoy as a couple, so the fertility treatment doesn't consume your relationship; and finally, take breaks when you need to. This is very important.

If you choose adoption or fostering then choose your agency wisely or try to get word of mouth recommendations. Do your research on adoption or fostering. Take a break from the process when you need to. Make sure you are both on the same page, otherwise cracks will appear later. Perhaps the chapters on our adoption experience will give you some insight into the process.

If you are wondering how our story ends, I will tell you. As I conclude this book, in 2018, I am twenty-eight years old and my husband is thirty-five. We have our whole lives ahead of us and the future will be bright, no matter what. At the moment we face childlessness, but this may change in time. We may be blessed with a miracle or we may choose to use two donors or adopt an embryo. For now we choose each other and life. We have chosen to be happy no matter what. We have ambitions which will come to bear fruit in time.

We wish to decorate our home and enjoy the happier atmosphere without the stress of infertility. We have our two cats, who will bring us years of happiness to come, and we are making new memories with our friends and family, enjoying new days out and hobbies. I will continue to be a voice for infertility and try to help others.

I want to end by saying that it has been an emotional journey for me writing this book. I would often write when I was feeling sad and particularly late in the evening, when all my worries would trouble me. I really hope this book helps others out there and gives you the feeling that you can be happy. Happiness will come. I wish you all one thing and that is happiness. I bet you thought I was going to say I hope you get your miracle baby, but the truth is happiness is the most important thing to wish for and, although it may not feel like that right now, it will come to you; and when it comes, happiness will be the most important thing, whatever form it comes in. So let me say it again; I wish you happiness ...

Z. Resources that helped me

- The Daisy Network - www.daisynetwork.org.uk/
- Positive Visualisation for IVF by Zita West (available on iTunes or CD format)
- Facebook support groups for infertility – Serum Athens IVF Support Group, UK IVF egg donors and recipients, Infertility Support UK, infertility support group.
- IVF and adoption books (the library was a great resource where I would borrow and read almost all of the books in these fields)
- Fertility counsellors
- Friends and Family
- Study on Hyuluronic acid binding - www.habselect.org.uk/index.html
- Fertility Network - www.fertilitynetworkuk.org
- Donor Conception Network - www.dcnetwork.org
- Endometriosis UK - www.endometriosis-uk.org

Printed in Great Britain
by Amazon